CROSS-CULTURAL
COMMUNICATION

CROSS-CULTURAL COMMUNICATION

Concepts, Cases and Challenges

Edited by
Francisca O. Norales

CAMBRIA
PRESS
Youngstown, New York

This book has been registered with the Library of Congress.
Norales, Francisca O.,
      Cross-Cultural Communication/Francisca O. Norales
      p. cm.
      Includes bibliographical references
      ISBN10: 0-9773567-3-6
      ISBN13: 978-0-9773567-3-7

To the memory of my mother, Francisca S. Norales (Belize, 1920–1994). A woman of courage, strength, and wisdom.

To my father, Felix A. Norales.

To my sisters, Yvonne and Geraldine.

To my niece, Sharanda, and nephew, Jovon.

CONTENTS

ACKNOWLEDGEMENTS

I am enormously grateful to my professors from Ball State University, Dr. Mollie B. Snyder and Dr. James H. McElhinney, who patiently molded, supported, and provided the foundation necessary for the realization of this volume. To the contributors who met the deadline dates, thanks for your patience.

My gratitude goes to the people who encouraged and created the atmosphere in which productive intellectual exchanges could occur. In particular, I acknowledge the support, efforts, and dedication of Dr. Paul Richardson, Publisher of Cambria Press for his graciousness in understanding my intentions. Thanks for your tremendous insights.

As always, my family has provided constant support, prodding me onward when I ran out of energy. Lest anyone should perceive of scholarly work as a solitary exercise, this collection is proof that it can be a productive, collaborative, and communicative endeavor.

Francisca 0. Norales

INTRODUCTION

This collection of essays, *Cross-Cultural Communication: Concepts, Cases and Challenges*, was conceived after learning of United Nations Educational, Scientific, and Cultural Organization (UNESCO) proclamations. It was on March 18, 2001 that UNESCO for the first time awarded the title, "Masterpieces of the Oral and Intangible Heritage of Humanity" to nineteen outstanding cultural forms of expression from different countries of the world. The criteria used in the selection process were outstanding value, roots in cultural tradition, affirmation of cultural identity, source of inspiration and intercultural exchange, contemporary cultural and social role, excellence in the application of skills, unique testimony of living cultural tradition, and risk of disappearing.[1] According to Roque (2002), the role of UNESCO in the field of languages is part of its efforts to protect intangible heritage just as tangible natural and cultural treasures are protected.[2]

Clearly, an urgent need for dialogue on topics such as communicating in a business environment, multicultural education, globalization, human rights considerations, and scholarly exchanges exists. Therefore, an attempt to initiate dialogue so that scholars can share their perspectives particularly on cultures that are rarely researched has been made.

A multicultural education is important to help students from diverse cultural groups attain the academic skills needed to function in a knowledge society. A multicultural education is an education for life in a free and democratic society. It helps students transcend their cultural boundaries and acquire the knowledge, attitudes, and skills needed to communicate effectively with those who are different from themselves.

The title, *Cross-Cultural Communication: Concepts, Cases and Challenges*, resulted from the realization of the close connection between the words "culture" and "communication." Anyone attempting to communicate with an international audience or with a culturally diverse colleague must consider one's cultural background. Cultural values influence how the world is viewed and how others are communicated with.

In the first chapter of this volume, I explore ways of communicating effectively in a multicultural workforce. Whether it is the events following the terrorist attacks of September 11, 2001, or the subway bombing in London on July 7, 2005, there is a strong motivation in many countries throughout the world as well as within organizations in the United States to improve intercultural and international relations through communication.

In chapter two, Sister Marie Lorraine Bruno draws on research in economics and international affairs to discuss the challenges associated with globalization. She highlights the importance of "language, the need for education, training, and possessing a sound ethical base as the qualities that are needed in the emerging world." The essay enables a reader to formulate his or her opinion in order to arrive at a creative solution.

In chapter three, Yash Garg contributes to understanding of Indian weddings, family, and festivals. She maintains that as a result of globalization, it has become imperative that a greater focus be placed on understanding other cultures. Yash Garg argues that it is the practice of core values, standards of conduct, customs and traditions that have been the unifying force of the Indian people. Additionally, family as an institution is perceived as the means through which cultural values are transmitted in India.

In chapter four, I examine the historical origin of the Garífuna culture of Belize, Central America which was recognized in United Nations proclamations. Some of the distinguishing characteristics of the culture such as the language, music, and dance are discussed.

In chapter five, Geraldine M. Norales and I discuss the historical evolution of the word "multiculturalism," and how the term is applied in Canada. Although there appears to be no precise agreement on the word, it does have connotations of "a public policy, an ideology, and cultural diversity." Workforce data pertaining to "Blacks," "all visible minorities," and "all Canadians" are included. In addition, the status of the African-Canadian in the workforce of Canada is discussed.

In chapter six, Concetta C. Culliver shows how police brutality such as the October 10, 2005 beating of Robert Davis in New Orleans can occur. She demonstrates that there is a massive breakdown in cross-cultural communication between the police and inner-city cultures. Concetta C. Culliver contends that racism is not the leading cause of white police officers' indifferent attitudes toward African Americans. Instead, she identifies "the lack of empathy and understanding for minority values and norms stemming from such disparate social and cultural backgrounds" as the primary cause of negative attitudes. In addition, she suggests a number of strategies to restore communication between the police and inner-city cultures.

In chapter seven, Concetta C. Culliver and I demonstrate that "globalization of knowledge" increases understanding and results in information-sharing across cultures throughout the world. Additionally, this type of globalization is beginning to play a significant role not only in the criminological theory process, but also in the development of American crime control policies. Furthermore, we discuss the fact that nations are dependent on one another for knowledge and information. For example, America's juvenile delinquency / justice system has been tremendously influenced by ancient Roman law and English common law. Clearly, nations are interdependent, culture does matter, and globalization is a reality!

Although the contributors to this volume have approached the subject of cross-cultural communication from diverse perspectives, common features have emerged from these discussions. As a result of globalization, the world has become smaller. There is no better time than now to understand cultures and cultural differences. The study of communication within cultures is important and research findings sometimes challenge commonly held assumptions.

The resilience of this group of contributors owes much to their diversity and their experiences which have allowed its members to adjust to the multicultural environments in which they find themselves. As editor, I recognize that much remains to be researched. This volume is propelled by an assertion that it is by exploring linkages among marginalized groups that attitudes, beliefs and values from ethnocentric epistemologies will be eradicated.

REFERENCES

[1] Retrieved June 27, 2001 from http://www.unesco.org/opi/intangible_
heritage/index.htm

[2] Roque, H. (2002, June–August). Will children inherit all out languages?
UN Chronicle 39 (2). [On-line]. Retrieved March 14, 2003 from
http://web5.infotrac-college.com/wadsworth/session/

CROSS-CULTURAL COMMUNICATION

SECTION 1
Communicating Within a Multicultural Workforce
Francisca O. Norales

More and more companies consider the diversity of human resources as an important, if not the most important, business issue. Companies such as Bell Atlantic, American Express, and Ford have implemented programs to address the issues and advantages of a culturally diverse workplace (Klimey, 1997). According to surveys conducted on the issue of workplace diversity, a resounding majority of businesses support and promote a more culturally diverse workforce (Pinkerton, 1995). This essay provides an understanding of the multicultural U.S. workforce, and analyzes the relationship between culture and communication.

The Importance of Effective Business Communication
The workforce in the United States is composed of people from Canada, the Caribbean, Latin America, Africa, India, and Asia. People from various ethnic backgrounds, such as African Americans, Caribbean Americans, Latin Americans and Asian Americans, bring their own language and culture to the workplace. Good communication is needed more than ever before in today's highly competitive marketplace. Today's consumers have greater knowledge of the value of various competing offerings. Effective communication may be the most important competitive advantage that firms have to meet diverse consumer needs on a global basis.

The global nature of our economy cannot be denied. An increasing number of companies have offices and factories around the world. To sell $200 million worth of appliances in India, Whirlpool adapts appliances to local markets and uses local contractors who speak India's several languages to deliver appliances. According to Arndt & Engardio (2001), Diebold manages and owns automated teller machines (ATMs) in Brazil, China, and France. In many countries in Latin America, consumers use banks to pay their utility bills, and Diebold's ATMs handle these services. According to Luo (2000), Otis Elevator's largest market is in China.

Challenges should be anticipated when people communicate within a single culture and a single country. These challenges increase exponentially when people communicate across cultures and countries. Succeeding in the global market today requires the ability to communicate sensitively with people from other cultures, a sensitivity that is based on an understanding of cross-cultural differences.

Exports are essential both to the success of individual businesses and to a country's economy as a whole. According to Edmondson (2000), two-thirds of all industries either already operate globally or are in the process of doing so. An increasing amount of profits comes from outside the headquarters' country. For example, Michelin earns 35% of its profits in the United States. McDonald's earns over 62% of its income outside the U.S. and almost 98% of Nokia's sales are outside its home country of Finland.

In a global economy, good ideas can emerge from other cultures and countries rather than from the headquarters. The chipmaker ST Electronics' Malaysian plant, headquartered in Europe, found a way to cut the assembly time for certain chips from five days to five hours. The company is currently transferring the technique to its Moroccan plant as well (Locker, 2003).

To fully understand how important communication is to the flow of business, the quantity of communication business requires should be noted. For example, within a pharmaceutical manufacturer, all employees throughout the company are involved in sending or receiving information. They process information with computers, write messages, fill out forms, give and receive orders, and converse over the telephone. In addition, salespeople receive instructions and information from the home office and send back orders and reports of their activities. Executives use written messages to initiate business with customers, other companies, and respond to incoming messages. Production supervisors receive work orders, issue instructions, and submit production summaries. Research specialists receive problems to investigate and later communicate their findings to management. Similar activities occur in every aspect of the company. Employees receive and send information as they perform their daily activities.

Oral communication is a major part of the flow of information within the work environment. So, too, are the various types of forms and records, as well as the storage and retrieval facilities provided by computers. In addition, newer forms of communication such as instant messaging, text messaging, email, and electronic files and reports are assuming a major role in the communication process.

Clearly, communication is essential to the organized effort involved in the business environment so that the goals of the organization can be achieved. Communication enables human beings to work together. Within a business environment, it is the vehicle through which management performs its basic functions. Managers direct, coordinate, plan, and control through communication.

Organizational communication once meant delivering information to selected audiences. Today, it means strategically addressing opportunities and needs so that the goals of an organization can be achieved. This means shaping messages and delivery mechanisms to connect with each regional, national, and international audience in ways that are timely, credible, and relevant.

Over the past five years, "offshoring," the sending of U.S. jobs overseas, has become an increasingly common business practice. According to Meisler (2004), savings can be obtained by outsourcing information technology and business-process tasks to vibrant emerging economies such as India. Other countries targeted for outsourcing efforts include the Philippines, China, Russia and Eastern Europe, and Central and South America.

Offshoring is not appropriate for every company. According to Meisler (2004), while most businesses survive the trip to another country, only a select few eventually achieve their financial targets. Many encounter numerous economic, managerial, political, and cultural problems along the way.

Because the Indian workday begins when the American workday ends, companies can conduct labor-intensive activities such as software testing at home and abroad, and save time by having the work continue around the clock. Although all educated Indians speak English fluently, a legacy of British colonialism, and are familiar with the American culture, misunderstandings still exist and must be confronted. Managers must be prepared to handle cultural differences, such as the importance of weddings in the Indian culture. During the three months perceived as the most auspicious time for weddings, up to half of the staff is expected to be out of the office (Meisler, 2004).

Diversity in the Workplace

There is a growing awareness that diversity in the workplace relates not just to gender and race but includes diversity associated with age, social class, regional differences, sexual orientation, and physical disabilities. Assisting each employee in reaching his or her potential requires more flexibility from managers as well as more knowledge about intercultural communication.

The last 15 years have seen a growing emphasis on diversity. The media reports that more women and people of color are joining the U.S. workforce. In fact, people outside mainstream cultures and power structures have always worked. For most of the country's history, hard working minorities were relegated to low-paying and low-status positions. Even after World War II when men from working-class families began to obtain college degrees in large numbers, and large numbers of women and minorities entered the professions in the 1960s and 1970s, few minorities made it into management. According to Clark (2000), U.S. businesses now realize that barriers to promotion not only harm employees but impede organizational success as well.

Research by Tyler (1990) shows that 40 million Americans (17% of the U.S. population) have disabilities making this the largest minority group in the United States. Disabled individuals are those who have difficulty thinking, moving, sensing, or emotionally coping. The following are suggestions when communicating with people who have disabilities:

- Place emphasis on the person and not the disability.
- Realize that people can have disabilities and may not necessarily be handicapped by them.
- Do not identify individuals by the disability; identify them as people.
- Use positive words to describe people with disabilities.

The Americans with Disabilities Act (ADA) has made it possible for individuals with disabilities to benefit from the same privileges afforded to workers in the U.S. In addition, the ADA has provided opportunities to encourage businesses to hire and facilitate the work of many talented people who were once deprived of access to employment. Organizations such as the Job Accommodation Network (JAN), a service of the President's Committee on Employment of People with Disabilities, are devoted to promoting the abilities and talents of employees with disabilities. JAN works with organizations in accommodating workers with disabilities, while at the same time putting qualified people to work (O'Hair, O'Rourke, & O'Hair, 2001).

Ways of Looking at Culture

According to Loden and Rosener (1990), a culture that fosters diversity is an institutional environment built on the values of fairness, diversity, mutual respect, understanding, and cooperation. The shared goals, rewards, performance standards, operating norms and a common vision of the future guide the efforts of every employee and manager. This trend is one of the major factors that have contributed to the importance of intercultural communication. Clearly, this cultural diversity affects how messages within organizations are planned, sent, received, and interpreted.

Each individual grows up in a culture that provides patterns of acceptable behavior and a belief system. In addition, a person may not even be aware of the most basic features of his or her own culture until that individual comes into contact with other people who do things differently. Similarly, every communication takes place in a social context, in verbal and non-verbal modes. Culture determines which mode predominates.

In a communication exchange where the message sender and receiver come from the same linguistic group and social background, there is more likelihood that both would attach the same meaning to the message. In some cultures, the message is clearly articulated in words, while in other cultures meaning is derived from the context of the communication.

Cultures are categorized as either high-context or low-context. In high-context cultures, most of the information is inferred from the context of a message; little is explicitly conveyed. Japanese, Chinese, Arabic and Latin American cultures are high-context. In low-context cultures, context is less important and information is explicitly spelled out. German, Scandinavian, and North American cultures are low context (Locker, 2003). Table 1 provides a summary of the differences between high- and low-context communication styles.

Table 1

Communication in High Versus Low-Context Cultures

	High-context (Examples: Japan, United Arab Emirates)	Low-context (Examples: Germany, North America)
Preferred communication strategy	Indirectness, politeness, ambiguity	Directness, confrontation, clarity
Reliance on Words to communicate	Low	High
Reliance on nonverbal signs to communicate	High	Low
Importance of written word	Low	High
Agreements made in writing	Not binding	Binding
Agreements made orally	Binding	Not binding
Attention to detail	Low	High

Source: Adapted from Victor, D. (1992). *International Business Communication*: 148, 153, 160.

In high-context cultures, the importance and power of words are not emphasized. The meaning of a message is less dependent on words. The perception of the message sender, including nonverbal cues, social and physical contexts, is used to attribute meaning to a transmitted verbal message. Statements may not be explicit. Additional information has to be filled in mentally by the message decoder. Therefore, a message encoder who relies heavily on words without regard to external cues may not communicate effectively across cultures.

In high-context cultures, verbs, metaphors, aphorisms, and anecdotes are often used when communicating. Silence is routinely used to deliver a message. According to Ferraro (1994), certain pronouns will be repeated frequently in order to fully dramatize the message, and highly graphic metaphors and similes are common. For example, it is not uncommon for an Arabic or a Garífuna speaker of Central America to use a list of adjectives to modify a single noun in order to stress a point (Norales, 2003). A statement may be overstated for emphasis, and the message receiver is expected to pick up the cues and make meaning out of them.

When conducting business in many cultures such as the Arab, African, and Caribbean, it is not uncommon to start a statement by expressing thanks to God or anticipating God's blessings in the future. This is often used to seek common ground and to affirm the omnipotent power of God among the participants during the communication transaction (Ihator, 2000).

Low-context cultures take written and oral communications literally. Contracts are binding. Promises may be "broken". In work environments, job tasks are separate from relationships. Individual initiative and decision-making are valued. Facts, statistics, and other details are emphasized. It is expected that the receiver of the message derives more of the meaning from the written or verbalized statements rather than from non-verbal behavioral cues. Business communication practices in the United States reflect these low-context preferences.

People of Diverse Ethnic Backgrounds

The United States has developed from the diverse values of Irish, African, Jewish, Hispanic, and Asian peoples (O'Hair, O'Rourke, & O'Hair,

2001). Unfortunately, many of these professionals find themselves balancing the values of their traditional culture against those of a contemporary white culture.The Mexican culture, for example, is characterized by traditional values such as cooperation and continual interchanges between people. If one member of a group should help with roof repair, another might return the favor by helping with, for example, childcare. Within the Garífuna culture of Central America, if one member of a group should help with renovations inside a home, another might return the favor by helping with renovations outside the home. The sharing of goods and labor is common for cultures with traditional values. In addition, decisions are made with the consideration of members of the group.

By contrast, competition is central to contemporary white cultures, and individual advancement is stressed. For instance, an Asian might feel uncomfortable listing accomplishments during an employee performance evaluation due to modesty. Clearly, the minority professional is often faced with competing values in the workplace.

According to O'Hair, O'Rourke, & O'Hair (2001), differing values also affect teamwork. People from cultures that view relationships in teams of hierarchy have a preference for highly structured teams. In contrast, people from cultures that see relationships in terms of groups prefer teamwork over a hierarchical focus. People from cultures that emphasize individualism are not comfortable with informal teams but prefer clearly defined groups and tasks. According to Riviera (1995), promoting the traditional values of other cultures in the workplace results in technical expertise, good human relations, teamwork, and a competitive edge in the marketplace.

Some general guidelines when communicating across cultures include:

- Realize that different cultures have different value systems.
- Do not assume that what is "normal" behavior in one culture is "normal" in another culture.
- Recognize that cultural differences exist in nonverbal behavior.

Nonverbal communication is ubiquitous. For example, one's smile or frown, who sits where at a business meeting, the size of an office, how long someone keeps a visitor waiting can communicate pleasure, anger, friendliness, distance, power or status. Most of the time, people do not consciously interpet nonverbal signals.

Nonverbal signals can be easily misinterpreted. These misunderstandings can be harder to clear up because people may not be aware of the nonverbal cues that led them to misunderstanding in the first place. For example, an Arab student felt that his U.S. roommate disrespected him because the U.S. student sat around the room with his feet up on the furniture with soles directed toward the Arab roommate. In general, Arab culture regards the foot, and the sole in particular, as unclean and the display of it an insult (Locker, 2003).

Avoid Stereotyping

Thoughts occur as people generalize about a variety of topics. A stereotype is one such generalization. Many are negative and inhibit communication because they are narrow and restrict people's perceptions of others. When people negatively stereotype others, they tend to take a few facts about an individual and apply those facts to everyone from that culture. In other words, a negative stereotype is a way of categorizing people by taking individual characteristics observed and generalizing them to all members of a culture. In many instances, these characteristics have not been observed, but were only based on other people's stereotypes.

When a stereotype is formed, a disservice to oneself as well as to that culture is done. In many instances, members of the stereotyped culture resent the generalization especially when the stereotypes are negative. Since prejudices are learned and developed, one must continually examine the basic assumptions about others who are different. Each individual should be considered on an individual basis and not stereotyped.

When business is conducted in other cultures, one should be aware of and examine stereotypes that may be held regarding individuals of the host country. Our goal should be to adapt to the ways of the host country and culture since we are the guests.

The Power of Language

Language is the key to the heart of a culture. So related are language and culture that language holds the power to maintain national or cultural identity. According to Edwards (1985), language is important in ethnic and nationalist sentiment because of its power and visible symbolism.

Because of the relationship between language and cultural identity, steps are often taken to prohibit the influence of other languages. For example, Costa Rica recently enacted a law that restricts the use of foreign languages and imposes fines on those who break it. Under the law, companies that advertise in a foreign language must also include a Spanish translation in larger letters. Likewise, France has a list of 3,500 foreign words that cannot be used in school, bureaucracies, or companies (Samovar and Porter, 2001).

Clearly, it is impossible to separate language from culture. According to Rubin (1992), language is a set of characters or elements and rules for their use in relation to one another. It can be discovered when studying another language that not only are the symbols (words) and sounds for those words different, but so are the rules (phonology, grammar, syntax, and intonation) for using those symbols and sounds.

Language is much more than just a symbol and rule system that permits communication with another person; it is also the means by which people think and construct reality. According to Nanda & Warms (1998), language does more than just reflect culture; it is the way in which an individual is introduced to the order of the physical and social environment.

Similarly, when a person chooses specific words to communicate, he or she is signaling membership in a particular culture or subculture by demonstrating that he or she knows the language. However, the language or vocabulary used imposes its own barriers on the message. For example, the language of a physician differs from that of an accountant, and the differences in their vocabularies affect their ability to recognize and express ideas.

Barriers also exist because words can be interpreted in more than one way. For example, to someone in the U.S., the word "catastrophe" can be used to describe a relatively small problem. In Belize, Central

America, the word is often taken literally to mean a hurricane. Clearly, words should be chosen with the audience in mind.

CONCLUSIONS

Succeeding in the global marketplace is an excellent way of expanding the capacity for businesses to grow. Several communication challenges should be expected when conducting business on the international level. Clearly, competent intercultural communication will be necessary in these global situations.

Cultural background plays a major role when communicating with international colleagues and with culturally diverse individuals in the United States. Cultural values influence how the world is viewed, and how communication occurs with others.

It is important that organizations strive to create a multicultural environment that values and preserves diversity. In addition, recognizing the cultural patterns of the world is a positive step in understanding the global marketplace. Employees must be prepared and trained to cope with cultural differences. Ultimately, cultural differences will be bridged through sensitiveness, flexibility, and awareness.

REFERENCES

Arndt, M. & Engardio, P. (August 2001). Diebold. *Business Week*, 138.

Clark, R. (2000, February). The future is now. *Black Enterprise*, 99.

Edmondson, G. (2000, August 28). See the world erase its borders. Business Week, 113.

Ferraro, G. (1994). *The cultural dimensions of International Business.* NJ: Prentice Hall.

Ihator, A. (2000). Understanding the cultural patterns of the World— An imperative in implementing strategic International PR Program. *Public Relations Quarterly* 45 (4), 38.

Klimey, A. (1997). Diversity programs: Coming of age. *Black Enterprise* 27, 115.

Locker, K. (2003). *Business and Administrative Communication.* Boston: McGraw-Hill/Irwin.

Loden, M. & Rosener, J. (1990). *Workforce America*. New York: Mc Graw-Hill, 196–197.

Luo, Y. (2000). *Partnering with Chinese firms: Lessons for international managers*. Burlington, VT, 217.

Meisler, A. (2004). Think globally, act rationally. *Workforce Management*, 83 (1), 40–42, 44–45.

Nanda, S & Warms R. (1998). Cultural *anthropology*. Belmont, CA: Wadsworth, Thompson Learning Inc.

Norales, F. (2003). The Garífuna Culture: A proclaimed masterpiece in Central America. *The Journal of Intergroup Relations* 30: 35–46.

O'Hair, H. O'Rourke, IV, J. & O'Hair, M. (2001). *Business Communication: A Framework for Success*. Cincinnati: South-Western College Publishing, a division of Thomson Learning.

Perkins, A. G. (1994). Diversity: "You say potato, and I say…" *Harvard Business Review*, 14.

Pinkerton, J. (1995). Why affirmative action won't die. *Fortune* 13, 191–198.

Rivera, M. (1995). Understanding cultural diversity. *Careers and the MBA*, 91–92.

Rubin, B. (1992). *Communicating and human behavior*. Englewood Cliffs, NJ: Prentice Hall.

Samovar, L. and Porter R. (2001). *Communication between cultures*. Belmont, CA: Wadsworth, Thompson Learning Inc.

Tyler, L. (1990). Communicating about people with diversity: Does the language we use make a difference? *The Bulletin* 53, 65–67.

Victor, D. (1992). *International Business Communication*. New York, Harper Collins.

Wayne, F. & Dauwalder, D. (1994). *Communicating in Business: An Action-Oriented Approach*. IL: Richard D. Irwin, Inc.

CHAPTER 2
The Challenge of Globalization
Sister Marie Lorraine Bruno

According to Hebel (2002), on September 11, 2001, the world did not change at all, our understanding of the world did. Many things have changed the world very rapidly, for instance, political changes such as the unification of Germany, or boundaries dissolved by the unification of the European nations, and the war in Iraq. It might be said that technological advances have been most effective in creating the borderless world, the global community. Thus, all peoples are faced with the challenge of understanding this world, the people who inhabit it, and their cultures.

This essay presents the advantages and risks of globalization. It does not attempt to solve the problems which the neo-liberal economy has caused the nations of the world, because there is still much unsettled controversy regarding globalization, which is many-faceted. The thoughts and opinions of leaders in the field of economics and international affairs are presented. This essay enables the discerning reader to formulate a well-informed opinion for a creative solution, and provides a deeper understanding of globalization and its effects upon the peoples of the world.

The Definition of Culture

According to Ferraro (1994), the only requirement for culture is to be human; therefore, the people in the world belong to a culture. Marzheuser (1995) stated that culture consists primarily of the symbols and stories people use to communicate their history and values. It is how they structure, organize, and creatively express their lives.

Additionally, culture provides order, identity and belonging. According to Hall (1976), culture is a word which stands for the sum of earned behavior patterns, attitudes, and material things. Culture is communication. It is not what people talk about but what people do along with the hidden rules that govern them. Riding (2004) stated that culture is a tool to integrate immigrants in their new environment. Immigration, a vital force in many nations, and a result of the borderless world, presents special problems. He further stated that there are few better tools of integration than culture, and that it empowers minorities, immigrants, and helps persuade nations that ethnic diversity is positive.

Cultural Communication

One who is engaged in global affairs of any kind must not forget the importance of language. Dawson (1967) stated that language lies at the root of culture, and that culture and language are inseparable aspects of the same process.

Victor (1992) noted that there are at least 2,796 languages spoken on planet earth. A person could never begin to learn all the critical languages of the world, but the person engaged in global affairs should have knowledge of the "critical language" of the people with whom business is being transacted. "Critical language" is defined as that which is not the native tongue of the speaker, but which is necessary for successful communication both verbally and nonverbally with a client, colleague or associate.

According to Hall (1976), cultural communications are deeper and more complex than spoken or written messages. The essence of cross-cultural communication might have more to do with releasing the right responses rather than sending the right messages.

THE IMPACT OF GLOBALIZATION

Webster's Seventh New Collegiate Dictionary (1964) defines intercultural as occurring between or relating to two or more cultures. With the rapidly changing world, international corporations have found it necessary to minimize the rate of misunderstanding due to miscommunication, either verbally or non-verbally. In the 1960s, organizations were training people of different cultures to get along with each other. In order to do so, one was trained for intercultural communication.

Webster's New World College Dictionary (1996) defines the word "globalize" as to organize or establish worldwide. However, globalization is more than international or transnational. It might be said that globalization dates from ancient times, or perhaps, from the beginning of modernity, the end of the 15th century. For the purposes of this essay, it should be considered a post-1945 occurrence whose driving force is technology, particularly telecommunications and computers. The recent trend is toward increasing the flow of goods, labor, materials, technology and funds between nations. It implies looking at the world as borderless, and perhaps, even without national identities. Goods, capital and personnel move freely, either in reality or by the use of technology. Information and communication travel quickly among the peoples of the world. For this to be done successfully, cultural diversity must be recognized, and appreciated. The true meaning of global is holistic, not international (Kanter, 1994, p. 230).

According to Anderson (2003), globalization has been called a "villain," and is causing most of the world's troubles. Those who are in agreement have noted the present unemployment rates in many countries including the U.S.A. Much is due to shifts in import / export trade. The U. S. exports less while companies overseas export more. Also, because technology plays an important role in globalization, it might be said that the wealthier countries "have the edge," and have created greater disparities of wealth among nations.

In discussing the economic, political and social effects, George & Welding (2002) noted that globalization requires low labor costs, gives multinational corporations (MNCs) control over the national economy, the society, and thus weakens the political system. On the other hand, centralized economies become decentralized when decisions are made by the MNC. Proponents claim that this can result in increased productivity, economic growth, and raises the standards of living.

DeMartino (2000) noted that in a global economy, an individual is free to improve or acquire new skills because in place of government allocations, MNCs reward employees for productivity. This can be disturbing because of the existential "I am what I do" attitude. It aids and abets the growth of a society which is moving rapidly to a dehumanized society. However, in answering the question whether this is just, DeMartino (2000) further stated that it is by rewarding contributions made to society that corporations will advance the collective interests of a society. His faith in this economy is unwavering, and is expressed as follows:

> ...until humankind evolves into some other form of creature than it is today, the free market economy is now and forever shall be best. As we overcome the remaining (formidable) obstacles to the perfection of the one-world economy, we will establish the conditions for a rising wave of prosperity and liberty the likes of which the majority of humanity has before enjoyed. We will bequeath to our children the basis for untold wealth, enduring peace, freedom and happiness. All they will need to do is complete the project we have pioneered. We will go to our grave having done far more than our fair share on behalf of those who will follow. We will have delivered humankind to the end of economic history (Ibid., pp. 9–10).

In response to this glowing, faith-filled approval of globalization, Bhagwati (2004), a champion of free trade, admitted that there are "possible downsides" and offered a "how-to" to make the "beneficial globalization" process work better. He requested establishing institutions and policies which will either eliminate the problems or allow societies to cope with them. He exhorted that optimal, not maximal speed of globalization, is to be achieved. He further stated that economic globalization affects poverty, child labor, women in the work force, and the environment.

According to Bhagwati (2004), economic argumentation and the empirical evidence do not lend support to the feared adverse link between child labor and globalization in the shape of trade. He further stated that although environmentalists claim that free trade is harmful to the environment, free trade must be combined with appropriate environmental policies and correct valuation of the environment.

In a video production, Ruiz (2001) discussed the crises of the global world, which were alluded to jobs, health care, education, social security, cultural values, the flow of immigrants across borders, the environment, and technology. Those victimized by globalization, as portrayed in the video, condemn the multinational corporations (MNCs), and claim exploitation. It can be argued that while the MNCs desire maximum economic gain, interest is generated in creating maximum social values. These corporations can be viewed as philanthropists in that they desire to meet the needs of customers throughout the world while they draw on the leadership, talent, and expertise of the host countries.

As an ultimate rejection, Bello (2002) stated that globalization is "corporation-dominated and a capital footloose." In addition, despite the ethical claim of producing the greatest good for people, the goal is profit. His strong condemnation that corporate-driven globalization as a process is marked by massive corruption, and is deeply subversive of democracy. He further articulated that globalization has not only lost its promise, but has embittered many nations.

According to Bello (2002), the context of discussion on deglobalization is based on the increasing evidence not only of poverty, inequality and stagnation that have accompanied the spread of globalized systems of production, but also of their unsustainability and fragility.

Given the rapid changes in the world today along with the increased influence of technology, in essence, "the ship has left the port," there is no returning. A new world will be reached beyond the horizon. Therefore, people must respond to the challenges with equity, justice, and ethical standards.

Changes in Organizations

A new "global logic" is emerging. Organizations are cosmopolitan especially since corporations today can have several worldwide headquarters. Consequently, there is growing awareness that workforce skills are critical. Ideas and talents are the capital of the 21st century. The quality of the work skills must be excellent in order to be competitive (Henzler, 1995). Companies including societies need well-educated workers who can think for themselves, solve problems creatively, and make decisions wisely. According to Victor (1992), a world where ignorance prevails cannot be a globalized world.

Several organizations including the U.S. government are cognizant of the necessity of providing training to personnel, and giving them the opportunity to develop and practice those skills when immersed in a second culture. The learner should be introduced to the root of her / his culture, that is, the language, both verbal and non-verbal, the political, social and economic factors prior to taking up residence in another country. This training is essential in order to reduce stress because of the psychological pressures associated with interaction with those of another culture. Perry (2004) noted the following discussion:

> Major Kirk Geiner: "We realize the importance of treating the Iraqis with respect and trying to gain their respect and trust" …
>
> Corporal Robert McNulty: "They're teaching us to respect the culture and not be so close-minded about things that are different" …

Globalization is making demands on the need of interpersonal skills in a new environment. Guy (1995) speaks of the "three (3) c's" and the "three (3) t's", which are basic to understanding other cultures. The three c's are as follows: 1) culture (background), 2) company style and 3) individual character. Similarly, the three t's are as follows: 1) tactics, 2) timing of activities, and 3) talking / listening. According to Page (1993), the trainer must be able to cope with the learner's resistance to adapt to defensiveness and frustration. Thus, one becomes aware of the emotional challenge that is encountered in the global community.

Emotional Challenges of Globalization

Stevenson (2004), noted that there are no foreign lands; it is the traveler only who is foreign. Such traveler would find it difficult to put herself or himself in the place of someone who is "different." People in the U.S. seem to have great difficulty in doing so. For example, the failure to trade with those of another culture, because it is expected that all peoples should conduct business the American way. Conducting business in the global community requires new interpersonal skills in a new environment. This tends to present a challenge because familiar activities will become unfamiliar. In extreme cases, one might try to hide one's insecurity when interacting with the other person. When this occurs, no human understanding can be present and no genuine interaction can take place.

According to Pells (2002), Americans have created "cultural imperialism," which has caused dislike for the U.S. In addition, since September 11, newspaper and magazine columnists and television pundits have said that it is not only the economic power of the U. S. or the Bush administration's "unilaterist" foreign policy that has resulted in global anti-Americanism. To a large extent, there is a lack of understanding of other cultures.

Also, other countries are experiencing emotional challenges. The fear that to globalize is to Americanize exists. Thus, national identities, cultures, heritages and the distinctiveness of nationalities are challenged and threatened with extinction. On the other hand, something that is worse than being "exiled" from one's native culture and identity is that of being held a prisoner by it, hence becoming provincial, insular, and perhaps, extinct (Ibid.).

Many countries are fearful of the hazards of the borderless world and the spread of infectious diseases such as AIDS, SARS, Mad Cow, and West Nile virus. In addition, the need to train or retrain for the highly technical jobs exists.

With the rapid transportation and communication systems, globalization has also challenged old standards, values, and morals, which are being "pressurized." These systems are moving so rapidly that the social, economic, political and ethical standards are shaken, at times so shattered that comparisons with the previous years are made. In order to decide which standard is better, time will be the determinant. However, it is worthwhile to reiterate the thought that globalization must be managed with equitable, just and ethical policies (Bhagwati, 2004).

Awareness of the Need to Globalize

There is awareness that globalization has to do with people, not nationalism. Ohmae (1995) stated that what matters is what people know, want or value, not the political or physical boundaries that might exist. Economic and social boundaries are affected by one's knowledge of how others live, what choices are made, and the value of those choices. He further stated that philosophical support from industrial democracies and public investment in education for responsible individual action and cultural diversity are the essence of a responsible, liberal, global economy. These educational resources will provide one with the ability to tolerate and show respect for pluralism.

Multinational corporations (MNCs) have moved to foreign facilities, are exporting from foreign facilities, and employing the natives of the foreign country. At the same time, there are non-U. S. companies in the U. S. who are creating more jobs for Americans. Companies have become global entities working anywhere in the world. Clearly, companies including employees in all levels must think globally.

Ohmae (1995) urged companies toward "insiderization," which meant giving local sovereignty to the endeavor in a foreign country. Each country requires its own relationship with the parent company. Thus, there is a real need to be sensitive to each group of people. A global company must learn how different countries are governed, how to work with those who govern, and how to satisfy the needs of the people.

According to the French-speaking television channel two, (2004), many foreign companies are experiencing great success through cultural adaptation strategies. A case in point is the French-owned company called Carrefour. While remaining French in name and selling French products, Carrefour was also selling Chinese products to the Chinese. Carrefour had "insiderized." Thus, workers must be knowledgeable, competitive, and possess work force skills. In speaking of a "didactic triad of cultural awareness," Hofstede, Pedersen, & Hofstede (2002) emphasized the importance of awareness of the social rules of society, knowledge of its cultural patterns, and skills in cross-cultural interaction.

The Importance of Language

Education, training, and possessing a sound ethical base are qualities that are needed for the emerging world. Basic to the knowledge of another culture is knowledge of its language. According to Bloch (1996):

> Language and culture are so firmly intertwined that optional cross-cultural international business cannot be attained without substantial foreign-language capabilities. Reasonable cultural awareness without foreign-language capabilities is common, especially among English-speaking business people, but such a lack of skills set very definite limits on the efficacy of cross-cultural performance (pp. 34–35).

However, speaking a second, third, or even a fourth language, does not guarantee that the learner will have a global perspective or attitude. That person may still be insular, nationalistic and narrow-minded. One with a global attitude is able to imitate other lifestyles, and also emerge as an enriched individual. A person with a global attitude may change but will not destroy a culture.

Legrain (2003) noted that "cross-fertilization" is essential to diversity and freedom. He further stated that the economic benefits of commerce are surpassed in importance by those of its effects which are intellectual and moral. It is hardly possible to overrate the value for the improvement of human beings of things which have brought them into contact with persons dissimilar to themselves and with modes of thought and action unlike those with which they are familiar. There is no nation that does not need to borrow from another.

In a global economy, the challenge of incorporating diverse populations, cultures and subcultures is experienced. All workers including the Chief Executive Officer (CEO) to the employee with the least significant responsibility must be educated accordingly to be able to solve problems and make decisions wisely. These decisions must be made with the intent of improving the quality of life for all. Thus, education with a strong ethical underpinning is essential. Such education provides understanding of different cultures, and results in true respect for other human beings.

The student of international business programs at the university level could profit from an internship experience abroad. According to Simon (1998), students should be encouraged, and ideally required to experience studying abroad. He further stated that if he could wave a magic wand, he would require foreign language study for all degree recipients. According to Baron (2001):

> America has a problem of linguistic security. We don't understand the languages of our attacker. Just a week after the Sept. 11 terror attacks, the Federal Bureau of Investigation was offering $38 an hour for translators of Arabic or of Pashto, the language of about 35 percent of the people of Afghanistan, including the Taliban. Many in Afghanistan, where bilingualism is widespread, understand both ...

> The weakness is not new. The FBI acknowledges that before the World Trade Center bombing in 1993 it had tapes, notebooks and phone taps that might have provided warning signs but it hadn't been able to decipher them because they were in Arabic. The first step in addressing our language deficiencies is a national recognition that they exist. If we really want to understand the words of our enemies — not to mention those of our friends — we need to put more emphasis on learning languages (p. A19).

Similarly, according to Meiland (2003):

> We're living in a special time, with our minds on war
> and terrorism, and we're losing sight of the reality of
> globalization. But we should pay attention, because
> national barriers are quickly coming down. If you look
> ahead five to ten years, the people with the top jobs in
> large corporations, even in the United States, will be
> those who have lived in several cultures and who can
> converse in at least two languages. Most CEO's will
> have had true global exposure, and their companies will
> be all the stronger for it. (p. 45).

Education and educators can offer the most effective solution to the challenge of globalization. According to Willen (2004), a group of business schools including the Wharton School, Harvard University, Northwestern University, the University of Michigan, Notre Dame University, the University of Minnesota, Pennsylvania State University and the University of Virginia in Charlottesville along with a group of corporate leaders are creating an institute for corporate ethics. This group is aware of the need to strengthen ethics requirements in their business programs. Given the problems in corporate America, and in the world today, a strong union between business and ethics in order to restore public trust is urgently needed. If the group is successful, they will affect not only national business endeavors, but also those on a global scale.

In questioning whether there should be a universal ethical standard, Grugal (2004), pointed out that values such as dependability and honesty travel a long way with anyone. He further stated that one thing that has strengthened his advocacy for a single worldwide standard of ethics is the global nature of business today. A company's reputation for integrity or the lack of it travels with that company wherever it does business.

CONCLUSIONS

Defining the word "globalization" is not an easy task. Often times, it is paradoxical, but surely, it is here to stay. It is both a fact and an opportunity. The challenges are not insurmountable. Solutions exist, and are waiting to be identified and implemented. Americans might need to lead the way. From a globalistic point of view, there is hope and faith in humanity. Given the proper education that fosters respect for all peoples, multinational corporations (MNCs) will begin to put people first.

There is hope and trust in those universities where courses such as business ethics are now core courses in the curriculum. Government should collaborate with MNC to accomplish the work to be done in training for cultural communication and to establish sound policies to protect people from the hazards and injustices of free trade as it is today. Americans will have to speak, interact and negotiate with others from another culture with ease, sensitivity, openness, respect and most importantly, with a strong ethical base. It is then that their efforts will be reciprocated.

REFERENCES

Anderson, G. (2003). Of many things. *America,* 189 (21), 2.

Badger, T. (2004, June 10). Labor gain in outsourcing: unions say recruiting is up. *Philadelphia Inquirer*, p. C1.

Bhagwati, J. (2004). *In defense of globalization.* NY: Oxford University Press.

Baron, D. (2001, October 27). America doesn't know what the world it is saying. *New York Times,* p. A19.

Bello, N. (2002). Deglobalization: Ideas for a new world economy. NY: Zed Books.

Bloch, B. (1996). The Language-culture connection in international business. *Foreign Language annals* 18 (1), 27–36.

Dawson, C. (1967). *The formation of Christendom,* NY: Sheed and Ward.

DeMartino, G.F. (2000). *Global economy, global justice.* NY: Rutledge.

Ferraro, G. P. (1994). The Cultural dimension of international business, NJ: Prentice Hall.

George, V. Welding, P. (2002). *Globalization and human welfare.* NY: Palgrave.

Green, S, Hassan, F., Immelt, J., Marks, M. & Meiland, D. (2003). In search of global leaders. *In Harvard Business Review*, Special issue. (pp. 38–45) MA: Harvard Business School Publishing.

Grugal, R. (2004, January 16). Be honest and dependable, values travel with you. *Investor's Daily*, p. A3.

Guy, V. & Mattock, J. (1995). *The International business book.* IL: NTC.

Hall, E. T. (1976). *Beyond culture*, NY: Doubleday.

_____. (1990). *Understanding cultural differences.* MA: Intercultural Press.

Hebel, S. (2002) Security concerns spur congressional interest in language programs. *The Chronicle of Higher Education* XLVIII (27), p. A26.

Henzler, H. A. (1995). The New era of Euro capitalism. In The *Evolving global economy.* MA: Harvard Business School Publishing.

Hofstede, G.T.; Pedersen, P.B.; and Hofstede, G. (2002). *Exploring culture.* ME: Intercultural Press.

Kanter, R. M. (1994). Afterword: What "Thinking globally" really means. In *Global Strategies: Insights from the world's leading thinkers*, (pp. 227–232). MA: Harvard Business School Publishing.

Legrain, P. (2003) Cultural globalization.is not Americanization. *The Chronicle Review* XLIX (35), B7–B10.

Marzheuser, R. (1995). Differing image of the church. *America* 173 (18), 17–21.

Meiland, D. (2003). In search of global leaders. In *The Harvard Business Review*, Special edition (pp. 38–45). MA: Harvard Business School Publishing.

Merriam-Webster (1964). *Webster's Seventh New Collegiate Dictionary.* MA: G. & C. Merriam Co.

NAFSA: Association of International Educators. (2003). Press Release Statement on the death of Paul Simon. Retrieved March 6, 2004 from http:// www.nafsa.org.

Ohmae, K. (1995). Managing in a borderless world. In Ohmae, K. (Ed.) *The Evolving global economy* (pp. 276–283). MA: Harvard Business School Publishing.

Page, R. (1993). *Education for the intercultural experience*. MA: Intercultural Press.

Pells, R. (2002) American culture goes global, or does it? *The Chronicle of Higher Education* XLVIII (31), B7–B9.

Perry, T. (2004, January 22) Troops learn Arabic Language and Arab ways. *The Philadelphia Inquirer*, p. A8.

Riding, A. (2004, July 24). French strive to be diverse without being less French. *New York Times*, p. B7.

Ruiz, W.R. (2001). The global generation beyond borders (video recording). Princeton, NJ: Films for the Humanities.

Simon, P. (1998). Point of View: Simon Says. NACUBO *Business officer.* Retrieved Marcy 6, 2004 from http://www.nacubo.org.

Stevenson, R.L. Retrieved January 15, 2004 from http://www.brainyquotes .com.

Victor, D.A. (1992). *International business communication*, NY: Harper Collins.

Willen, L. (2004, January 15, 2004). Business ethics institute planned. *The Philadelphia Inquirer*, p. C3.

CHAPTER 3
Representing Culture: Indian Weddings, Family, and Festivals
Yash Garg

> Though outwardly there was diversity and infinite
> variety among our people, everywhere there was that
> tremendous impress of oneness, which had held all of
> us together for ages past, whatever political fate and
> misfortune had befallen us. (Nehru, 1946, p. 47).

In the present day world of rapid globalization, it is becoming
increasingly imperative for more countries to have understanding of
other cultures. The Chinese and Indian cultures have become all the
more important because together they represent more than two billion
people. While it is true that India is a land of extremes and contrasts,
thereby making it very difficult to generalize, there are areas in which
disagreements are few. To enable understanding of Indian behavior
patterns, this essay concentrates on the commonalities in Indian traditions
and celebrations rather than their differences in regard to weddings,
family, and festivals.

Geography
A democratic republic in the southern part of Asia, India borders Pakistan
in the northwest, China and Nepal in the north, and Bhutan, Bangladesh,
and Myanmar (once called Burma) in the northeast. The southern part of
India is a peninsula, or land surrounded by water on three sides. The Arabian
Sea lies to the west, the Bay of Bengal to the east, and the Indian Ocean
to the south.

India consists of three main regions which are as follows: the
mountainous north, the plains, and the peninsula. Each region has a
different geography and climate. Part of the Himalayan Mountains in
northern India have the highest peaks in the world. Winters in the

mountains are very cold, while summers are warm and dry. South of the foothills of the Himalayas, the land levels off to form the northern plains. The hot and dry Thar Desert lies in the northwestern part of the plains, but to the east the land is well watered. It is from this area that three major rivers flow: the Brahmaputra, the Indus, and the Ganges. The waters of the Ganges are sacred to the Indian people. Because of the abundance of water and rich soil, the northern plains region of India is the most densely populated area of the nation (Cifarelli, 1996). India is the seventh largest country in the world; by area it encompasses 1,269,419 square miles or 3,287,782 square kilometers. By population, it ranks the second largest country in the world, crossing the one billion mark at the turn of the new millennium.

The Indus Valley Civilization
The name "India" derived originally, through the Persians and the Greeks, from the region of the great river Indus (or Sindhu). Europeans called the peninsula the Indies and the Spice Islands. By retaining the name India upon independence in 1947, the Indian people claimed and inherited an ancient and rich history and culture (Watson 1975:11).

A BRIEF ANCIENT HISTORY OF INDIA
India's civilization began around 2,500 B.C., in the valley of the Indus River. Archaelogists discovered ruins of marvelous ancient cities at places now called Harappa and Mohenjo-Daro. According to the buildings, streets, and tools found at the cities, the Indus Valley civilization was very advanced. The people even had a system of writing, although experts have not been able to translate it (Cifarelli 1996:14).

In 1750 B.C. the Indus Valley civilization came to an end. For reasons that are not known, the great cities were abandoned, and people began to live in simple villages. A people from the northwest called the Aryans started to move into northern India. Many of the traditions that the Aryans brought are still part of Indian life. Today, descendants of the Aryans can be found in the northern half of India, and the indigenous Dravidian, in the south (Watson, 1975).

After the arrival of the Aryans, India was divided into many small kingdoms, which were often at war. However, a few brilliant rulers were successful in uniting large regions. These kings founded powerful dynasties and ruled great empires with some dynasties lasting for centuries. According to Cifarelli (1996), the first great dynasty in India was the Maurya, which rose to power around 320 B.C. By 273 B.C. the Maurya dynasty controlled vast reaches of lands. The empire stretched from Central India to the area that is now Afghanistan in the northwest.

Five hundred years later, another great dynasty called the Guptas arouse. The Guptas ruled from A.D. 320 to 550, conquered much of northern India, and had power over nearly the entire subcontinent.

Following the downfall of the Mauryas and the rise of the great Gupta dynasty, the intervening period was of great significance. In the Gangetic valley, the orthodox Hindu tradition re-established itself under the local dynasties and Sanskrit literature witnessed a revival which was to have far-reaching consequences. In the area between the plains of Hindustan and the Deccan plateau a new dynasty known as Satavahanas established itself as a great power. Placed as they were between the Dravidian of the south, and the Aryanized Hindustan, they were able to create a basic cultural unity for the entire country of India (Panikkar, 1965).

The British in India

On December 3, 1600, the "Governor and Company of Merchants of London Trading into the East Indies" was chartered by Queen Elizabeth. Over 200 Englishmen had contributed close to £70,000 as the initial capital behind this venture. The royal charter granted Governor Thomas Smythe and his 24 "committees" of London merchants a monopoly on all trade between the Cape of Good Hope and the Straits of Magellan for 15 years. Four ships were outfitted the following year, a beginning for what became the administrative agency of Britain's empire in India (Wolpert, 1965).

The first half-century of British contact with India was an era of meager mercantile expansion in which British expectations of grandiose profits were frustrated by Dutch and Portuguese competition as well as Mughal indifference. According to McNair (1990), the founder of the Mughal Empire was a Muslim king named Babar who invaded India in 1526. He was part Mongol and originated from Afghanistan. Following Babar, seven generations of Mughal emperors extended their territories until they included northern India, Afghanistan, present-day Pakistan and Bangladesh, and much of southern India.

Denied equality of trade, the British merchants were content to linger in India by the grace of Mughal, and eagerly took advantage of serving the Mughals whenever the opportunity presented itself. Surat became the first center of British interest in India until 1687 when it was superseded by Bombay (Ibid., p. 69).

According to Cifarelli (1996), in 1857 the British conquered the entire country of India and made it part of the British Empire. The Indians, however, felt discriminated against in their own land and consequently struggled for independence.

Independence

After World War II, it became obvious that the British could not justify their presence in India. Consequently, in 1948, the British government appointed Lord Mountbatten as the viceroy who would preside over India's independence. On August 15, 1947, India became an independent country with Jawaharlal Nehru, Gandhi's greatest follower, as its first prime minister.

GLOBALIZATION OF IDEAS

Philosophical thoughts have traveled back and forth between India and English-speaking lands with each influencing the other. Trading ships made regular voyages between American colonies and India for many years before the American Revolution. Diplomatic relations were established by President George Washington who sent an American consul to Calcutta in 1782 (McNair, 1990). On the other hand, Great Britain played a long and significant role in the history of India. In turn, India's modern leaders were influenced by British and American thoughts. Mahatma Gandhi, the Indian hero who deserves most of the credit for leading his country to independence, used nonviolent resistance to tyranny and oppression. His ideas were influenced by both the Hindu religion and the writings of the American essayist, Henry David Thoreau.

In the 1960s, the American Civil Rights Movement derived much of its inspiration from India's experience. The movement's leader, the Reverend Martin Luther King, Jr., visited India, met with Prime Minister Nehru, and studied Gandhi's methods intensively. Dr. King's birthday is noted each year in India with newspaper editorials that point out what the two countries learned from one another in their struggles for freedom.

THE DEFINITION OF CULTURE

In 1699 B.C., the Aryans came from Central Asia and dominated the Indian subcontinent both militarily and culturally. The term "Aryan" meant "pure," and signified the invaders' conscious efforts to show their superiority to the Dravidians, the earlier inhabitants of the subcontinent. The Aryans brought with them a new language, Sanskrit, a new pantheon of gods, and a patriarchal family system. It is noteworthy that the Indian word for culture is "sanskriti," which means refined and cultivated, as opposed to "prakrti," which means inherent or instinctual. Whereas nature is immutable, culture is learned or acquired by virtue of membership in a society or community. According to Tylor (1958), culture is "that complex whole which includes knowledge, belief, art, morals, law, custom and any other capabilities and habits acquired by man as a member of the society." The Indian culture known today, emerged from the fusion of Aryan and Dravidian traditions, beliefs and value systems. It is the practice of the core values, standards of conduct, customs and traditions that have been instrumental in unifying the Indian people despite their great diversity.

PHILOSOPHY

Religion, The Four Castes, Stages, and Ends of Life

According to Ganeri (2001), three-quarters of all Indians are Hindus. They believe in a supreme being called Brahman, whose various characters are represented by three main gods which are as follows: 1) Brahman (the Creator); 2) Vishnu (the preserver); and 3) Shiva (the destroyer). Existing within the Indian culture are thousands of other gods and goddesses (Ibid., p. 5). Additionally, some people worship in temples, while others in small shrines in their homes. Since Hinduism is an extremely flexible religion, some Hindus do not perform any formal worship. Imbedded within Hinduism is the belief in reincarnation and for Hindus the ultimate goal is "moksha," or salvation from the cycle of birth and rebirth. Other major religions include Islam, Buddhism, and Sikhism (Ibid).

Indian society divided its people into four "varnas" or castes, and life is divided into four "ashrams" or stages, with specific duties assigned to each.The Sanskrit phrase "varnaashramadharma" is indicative of this concept that each varna and ashram has its distinct set of duties.

Originally, the caste system was the way of division of labor among the Indian people. It was a person's occupation or profession that determined his or her caste. According to Risabhchand (1964), the caste system was based on the following Indian idea:

> [M]an falls by his nature into four types. There are, first and highest, the man of learning and thought and knowledge; next, the man of power and action, ruler, warrior, leader, administrator; third in the scale, the economic man, producer and wealth getter, the merchant, artisan, cultivator." And the last type, he adds, belongs to the Sudras, who are "fit only for unskilled labor and menial service. (Rishabhchand, 1964, pp. 39–40).

As the Indian sociologist Motwani (1947) puts it, caste division "insured efficiency and economic strength and promoted social integration ... The functional castes, like the mediaeval guilds of Europe, fostered esprit de corps, encouraged due recognition of mutual bonds of interdependence."

One of the main sources of information about Aryan religion are a collection of 1,028 hymns called the Rig Veda. These were recited by priests at sacrifices and ceremonies. Some hymns were addressed to specific gods; there are also battle hymns, observations, and dialogues. Hymns from the Rig Veda are still sung at weddings and funerals (Ganeri, 2001).

The caste is mentioned in the tenth book, Hymn XC of the Rig Veda. It conceives of the society as a giant body, with the Brahmins (priests, thinkers and scholars) as the head, the Kshatriyas (warriors and rulers) as the arms, the Vaishayas (businessmen and farmers) the thighs, and Sudras (menial and unskilled workers) as the feet. Each caste had its function in sustaining and nurturing the health of the social body. At first, one could change one's profession and caste, but over time, the caste system became a bane of the Indian society as it became rigid and hereditary.

According to Nehru (1960), the Kshatriya caste "depended more on status and occupation rather than on descent, and so it was much easier for foreigners to be incorporated into it." While many great people of India have warned against the rigidity of the caste system, Mahatma Gandhi recognized the need for its elimination. According to Gandhi, "Caste must go if we want to root out untouchability." Today, caste discrimination is illegal, though it has yet to be eliminated from social practice. Under the influence of modern ideas of enlightenment, people in India are free to choose their professions in spite of the caste into which they are born. Inter-caste marriages are on the rise in India and are the order of the day among the people of the Indian Diaspora.

Manu, the Indian lawgiver, divides life into four *ashrams* (stages), each with its own set of duties and observances. According to Manu Smiriti (Law Code of Manu), the four stages are as follows:

I. Life as a "Vidyarthi" or student;
II. Life as a "Grihasthi" or householder;
III. Life as a "Vanprasthi" or spiritual aspirant; and
IV. Life as a "Sanyasi" or preacher.

Each stage is accompanied by its own *dharma*, or duty. Manu asserts that after "having spent the first fourth of his life in the house of his guru, the second fourth in his own house with his wife, the third part in forests, that one should take sanyasa in the fourth part casting away every worldly tie."

Indian traditional culture is based on four main ends of life, namely: "dharma" or cosmically-ordained duty; "artha" or gainful employment or worldly success; "kama" or enjoyment of physical or sensual pleasures; and "moksha" or salvation or liberation from the cycle of births and deaths.

The term "dharma" is derived from the Sanskrit root "dhr," which means to bear or to hold. The Hindu Scripture states that "this world is upheld by Dharma." According to Monier-Williams (2005), Dharma is that which is established or firm, steadfast decree, statute, ordinance or law; usage, practice, customary observance or prescribed conduct or duty; right, justice (often as a synonym for punishment); virtue, morality, religion, religious merit or good works.

According to Zaehner (1966), "verily, that which is Dharma is truth." In other words, dharma is not just law, but it is the only "Sat" or Truth. Dharma thus represents not only the established law and order, but it also encompasses the duties of humans in general as well as the duties of individuals in all matters, both sacred and secular. Dharma guides a person to righteous conduct at all times and at all stages of life. The problem of finding one's dharma in difficult situations is one of the primary themes of the Bhagvad Gita, which is considered to be as sacred to the Hindus as the New Testament is to Christians. The Bhagvad Gita or The Lord's Song, is included in an epic where Lord Krishna expounds his duty to Arjuna when the latter lays down his arms and faces a moral dilemma as to whether he should fight his evil cousins (Roy, 1927–32). Arjuna learns that he must fight the evildoers, no matter who they are. Lord Krishna proclaims that he incarnates himself whenever dharma is in danger and runs the risk of being destabilized.

WEDDINGS, FAMILY AND FESTIVALS

Weddings, family, and festivals perhaps best represent Indian culture. After a person completes his or her life as a student, he or she is ready to enter the most important stage of the householder. The Code of Manu considers this stage to be the prop of the social structure: "Just as all creatures exist depending on air, so do all the Ashrams depend upon the householder. Because the householder supports the three orders by means of knowledge and food, so his order is the highest." A wedding is the greatest event in an Indian family, and it is one that involves much expenditure and social obligations for the families of the bride and the groom. While most marriages are still arranged through parents who introduce the couple, marriages in which the partners choose each other are increasingly becoming common. However, marriage in India is not between just two individuals, but also between their families.

At one time, it was common for the bride's parents to give a dowry upon marriage. Unfortunately, some parents demanded exorbitant amounts from the bride's parents for the education of their son. There have even been cases of a particularly horrifying type of domestic violence, such as bride burning, when a bride's parents could not satisfy the dowry demand. Today, demanding a dowry is illegal under Indian law.

Ceremony

Whereas wedding rituals vary from region to region, a practice that is common to an Indian wedding ceremony, or "Vivaha samaskara, " is the circumambulating of the sacred fire four times. In walking around the fire, the bride and the groom proclaim their desire to achieve the aforementioned goals of dharma, artha, kama, and moksha in their married life. The couple alternates by leading each other around the fire, symbolizing that each can take the responsibility for directing the course of their life together. At each round, they stop to touch a stone in their path symbolizing the obstacles that they will encounter and overcome together. Another important ritual is that of "saptapadi" or seven steps and vows. These steps represent seven promises that are made to one another. They are as follows:

- To cherish each other in sickness and health, happiness and sorrow;
- To respect each other's families as his or her own;
- To remain faithful to each other forever;
- To stand by each other in sadness and rejoice in happiness;
- To complement and complete each other;
- To share everything God has blessed each with; and
- To acknowledge that God is a witness to the wedding.

Family

Family is the single most important institution in India for the purposes of transmitting cultural values. For many years the joint family was the order of the day in India, when sons brought their brides to live jointly in their father's home, and shared work and income, pleasures and comforts, as well as troubles and tribulations with other members of the extended family. Today, nuclear urban families are quite common, especially among young professionals. The Indian family celebrates joyous occasions, events, and festivals as a unit. Living in a joint family gives the members a sense of protection and security. Parents teach children their duties toward their siblings, to help one another in times of distress and crisis. Indian epics are replete with examples of wifely devotion, a son's sacrifice to honor his father's words, and sibling devotion. The role of a mother in the family is central as she is the one who teaches her children cultural values and traditions.

Rama and Sita, the hero and the heroine of the Hindu epic Ramayana, are considered role models of a man and a woman. Rama unhesitatingly agrees to go into exile for fourteen years to honor his father's word, but his wife Sita, refuses to remain at home at her husband's bidding, declaring, "[A] wife enjoys the fortune of her husband since she is a part of himself... Assuredly, I shall accompany thee to the forest uninhabited by men, filled with savage beasts, such as bears and bulls." By calling herself "a part" of her husband, Sita is here emphasizing the Indian belief that a husband and a wife complement each other and must share each other's joys and sorrows (Shastri, 1952). According to Zaehner (1966), "oneself is like half of a split pea," thus underscoring the mutual dependence of men and women in married life.

A typical Indian family shares their joys and sorrows as a unit. Births, deaths, and marriages are family events. Also, family honor is a matter of paramount importance. The word given must be honored even at the cost of one's life. At times, a son may sacrifice his own comforts and happiness for the sake of his younger siblings. When a family member falls on hard times, others join hands to help him or her in any way possible. Prayers for the peace of ancestral souls are, however, recited by the oldest son. The ceremony of "Shraddha" or annual rites for the departed souls is performed by all male descendants to honor three generations of deceased ancestors. Special gift items and clothing are also donated to the officiating priest.

The Status of Women

The position of a wife in ancient India seems to have been high, as is evident from the Indian term for a married couple, "dampati," which means "co-rulers." However, over time, the position of the Indian woman progressively deteriorated, and it was at its lowest when the British arrived in India. Polygamy and child marriage were permitted. The custom of Suttee (wife's burning herself on her husband's funeral pyre) was practiced in northern India, especially among members of the warrior class of Rajputs; widow remarriage was also not allowed among members of the upper castes.

In 1927, the All-India Women's Conference was founded, and this organization sought to improve women's social and economic status. Women were an integral part of the independence struggle led by Mahatma Gandhi. They participated in Gandhi's Salt March in 1930, and as many as 17,000 women courted arrest. Indian women gained more equal rights with men only after India's independence. The Hindu Marriage Act of 1955 prohibits polygamy and child marriage and provides for both separation and divorce. The Adoption and Maintenance Act of 1956 gives women the right to adopt children. Perhaps the most revolutionary of these new laws concerning women's rights is the Hindu Succession Act of 1956, which accords women the right to inherit property, and daughters, mothers, and widows the right to share equally with sons the self-earned property of the man who dies without a will (Lamb, 1966).

Among the few emancipated Westernized minority are many outstanding and forceful women prominent in public life. The most notable example is India's third Prime Minister, Mrs. Indira Gandhi (not related to the Mahatma), the first woman in modern times to become the chief executive of a major power. Before becoming prime minister, Mrs. Gandhi had an active career in social welfare and in Congress Party politics, serving as president of the party in 1959–60 (Lamb, 1968). According to Blackwell

(2004), this positive move may indicate that class and family in India are more important than gender (p. 150). Certainly, Mrs. Gandhi had to have personal strength to win her battles. Today, women in India can be found in various levels of the society. Many have taken up the fight for women's causes, and they include lawyers, physicians, educators, journalists and professionals in other fields.

Festivals

Festivals keep Indian people connected to their cultural roots, give them an opportunity for emotional and spiritual renewal, and help them follow dharma or the path of duty. The approach of a festival prompts Indian people to clean their homes. Women decorate the doorsteps of their homes with creative designs called "rangoli," using sand, grains, or paints. Women also decorate their hands with "mehandi," or henna designs, to show to relatives and friends. Because different festivals are celebrated across the country, the focus is on a few representative festivals like Vasant Panchmi and Holi, which bring out the community spirit and cultural unity of Indian people; festivals like Raksha Bandhan and Karwa Chauth, which strengthen sibling affection, and spousal love, respectively; and above all, the festival of Diwali, when Indians light their homes with clay lamps and candles, and take stock of their works during the year and make new resolutions for the year to come.

Vasant Panchami is the festival that heralds the advent of spring, and marks the end of winter. "Vasanta" means the spring season. According to the Indian almanac, this festival falls in the month of Magh (January–February). Just as the Irish wear green clothes on St. Patrick's Day, Indians welcome the onset of spring by wearing yellow, and coloring food yellow with saffron. The festival commemorates the burning of the god of love, Kamadeva, by Lord Siva. When Kamadeva awoke Lord Siva from deep meditation with arrows, Lord Siva opened his third eye and reduced the god of love to ashes. This is the reason Kamadev is called Ananga, the one who is without a body. Apart from its religious meaning, this story points to the invigorating power of the spring season. The day is celebrated outdoors with wrestling matches, kite flying competitions, and poetry recitals.

While the northerners of India refer to the festival as Vasanta Panchmi, the Bengalis refer to it as Saraswati Puja Day. On this day, they worship Saraswati, the goddess of learning, and hold literary competitions. Also on this day, Bengali children start their education in order to receive the blessings of the goddess of learning. In olden days, dramas of great writers like Kalidasa were enacted on this festival. In the evening, devotees take images of Saraswati in procession and immerse them in the river.

The month of March brings Holi, the festival of colors and mirth. One of the most popular of the Indian festivals, Holi is celebrated throughout India with tremendous gusto and fervor. On the Holi eve, people make bonfires in public squares. People from all sections of the Indian society, the young and old, rich and poor celebrate this festival by throwing colored powder or colored water on friends and relatives.

The festival of Raksha Bandhan, which falls on the full moon day of the Indian month of Shravana (August), reaffirms the bond between brothers and sisters. The phrase "Raksha Bandhan" means "Promise to Protect." On this occasion brothers renew their pledge to come to their sisters' help in times of need, and sisters pray for their brothers' good health and prosperity as they tie "Rakhis" or decorative threads around the right-hand wrist of their brothers. According to Hinduism, when Indra, the king of gods, began to lose in the war against demons, his wife Indrani tied the sacred thread to Indra's right-hand wrist, and consequently, turned the tide in Indra's favor. The rakhi serves as a two-fold blessing. It is meant to protect the brother against evil, and the brother in turn is obligated to defend his sister whenever the need arises. This festival thus reinforces the affection between brothers and sisters as well as their duties toward each other. It is customary for the brothers to give their sisters money or gifts such as clothing or jewelry as tokens of their love. Sisters living abroad likewise send "Rakhis" by mail to their brothers, who in turn send gifts to their sisters.

Karwa Chauth festival falls in the month of Kartik (October–November), and comes nine days before Diwali, the most popular of the Indian festivals. It is observed in the northern and western parts of India. The term "karwa" means an earthen pot with a spout, symbolic of peace and prosperity, and "chauth" means the fourth day of the new moon. On this day, married women pray for the longevity and well being of their husbands. They arise very early, generally before the dawn of day, perform their ablutions, wear new clothing, and partake of a meal of select grains and fruits. For the remainder of the day, they abstain from food and drinks, and break the fast only after seeing the moon. Women wear their best clothes and ornaments for the occasion, and adorn their hands with intricate mehandi (henna) designs. Of course, all wives expect lavish gifts from their husbands. It is noteworthy that in the event the wife should become ill, her husband may keep the fast for the well-being and longevity of the couple. From personal experience, my father-in-law kept the fast when my mother-in-law became ill. This festival aims at promoting spousal love and sets the tone of festivity and feasting for Diwali.

"Deepavali" or "Diwali," which literally means a row of lamps, is the most important of Indian festivals. Diwali night is a sight to see with all homes and buildings glittering with lights. Diwali is celebrated throughout India and wherever the Indian Diaspora can be found. Like Christmas, Diwali is a national holiday, and all Indian people, irrespective of rank and status, are imbued with a festive spirit.

Every year, Diwali falls on a different date in October or November because Indians follow the lunar calendar in matters of festival dates. Diwali celebrates the victory of forces of good over those of evil. It celebrates the slaying of the demon Narkasura, as well as the victory of Lord Rama over the demon Ravana, with Rama's triumphant return to his capital of Ayodhya with his consort Sita and brother Lakshmana after fourteen years in exile. Traditionally, people would light clay lamps filled with mustard oil, but candles and electric lights are increasingly popular, illuminating windows, balconies, and roofs of houses. Dressed in their best clothing, celebrants visit friends, relatives, with sweets in their hands. On Diwali people worship Lakshmi, the goddess of wealth and prosperity. They clean and decorate their homes with Rangoli designs to make them suitable for a visit from Lakshmi.

Also, Diwali marks the beginning of the New Year, at which time merchants close old ledgers in order to start new ones. In short, Diwali is the day of national rejoicing and festivity, annual stocktaking, as well as prayers for prosperity and happiness for the New Year.

In addition to the salient features of common culture, Indians believe in the philosophy of Karma, according to which an individual's actions performed in this life and in the earlier incarnations, determine the individual's status and fortune. According to the most popular sacred book, the Bhagavad Gita, an individual's duty lies in action only, and not in the fruits of the action. Doing duty for duty's sake should be the primary concern of an individual in action. "Mukti" or salvation is available to all souls, and no soul will suffer in hell forever, although a soul may experience numerous births and deaths to attain salvation.

CONCLUSIONS

The history of India since independence has many achievements. Though a republic, India elected from the beginning of independence to remain within the Commonwealth, thus maintaining relations with the United Kingdom. India maintained a culture which has given significance to its history.

The primary focus of Indian culture is the promotion of dharma as it relates to the individual's life, family, society and the world at large. All cultural activities, observances, ceremonies and celebrations are performed to uphold dharma.

Whether one performs a series of rites and celebrations, from baby shower to "shraddha," or participates in family traditions and festival celebrations throughout life, one is expected to support and sustain dharma. In the final analysis, Indian cultural acts are geared toward strengthening family relationships, as well as promoting unity among the Indian people.

REFERENCES

Basham, A. L. (Ed.) (1975). *A cultural history of India.* New York: Oxford University Press.

Blackwell, F. (2004). *India: A global studies handbook.* Santa Barbara, CA: ABC-CLIO, Inc.

Cifarelli, M. (1996). *India: One nation, many traditions.* New York: Marshall Cavendish Corp.

Chopra, P. N. (Ed.) (1984). *An encyclopaedic survey.* New Delhi: S. Chand and Company.

Edgerton, F. (Trans.) (1972). *The Bhagavad Gita.* Cambridge, MA: Harvard University Press.

Gandhi, M. K. *The collected works of Mahatma Gandhi.* (1958–1994). (100 Vols.). Delhi: Publications Division, Ministry of Information and Broadcasting,Government of India.

Ganeri, A. (2001). *Exploration into India.* Philadelphia, PA: Chelsea House Publishers.

Garg, Y. (1999). "Regenerative rituals." In w*holeness and holiness.* NC Crossroads, 2.

Heitzman, J., and Worden, R. L. (Eds.) (1996). *India: A country study.* Washington, DC: Federal Research Division, Library of Congress.

Husain, S. A. (1963). *Indian culture.* New York: Asia Publishing House.

Kriplani, J. .B. (1991). *Gandhi: His life and thought.* New Delhi: Publications Division.

Lamb, B. P (1968). *India: A world in Transition (*3rd ed.). New York: Frederick A. Praeger, Publishers.

Lamb. (1966). *India: A world in Transition* (2nd ed.). New York: Frederick A. Praegar, Publishers.

Monier-Williams, M. (2005). *Brahamanism and Hinduism.* Kila, MT: Kessinger Publishing.Company.

Motwani, K. (1947). *India: A synthesis of cultures.* Bombay: Thacker & Co.

Mc Nair, S. (1990). *Enchantment of the World: India.* Chicago, IL: Childrens Press, Inc.

Nehru, J. (1946). *The discovery of India.* New York: John Day Company.

Panikkar, K.M. (1965*).* The history of India. In E. Fodor & W. Curtis (Eds.), *Fodor's Guide to India* (pp. 116–135). New York: David McKay Co., Inc.

Radhakrishnan , S. and Moore, C. (Eds.) (1957). The laws of Manu. In *A source book in Indian philosophy.* Princeton, N.J: Princeton University Press.

Risabhchand, S. (Compiler). (1964). In S. Aurobindo. *The message and mission of India.* Chowpatty, Bombay: Bhartiya Vidya Bhavan.

Roy, P. C. (Trans.) (1927–32). *The Mahabharata* (11 Vols.). Calcutta: Oriental Publishing Company.

Shastri, H. P. (Trans.). (1952). *The Ramayna of Valmiki.* London: Shanti Sadan.

Tharoor, S. (1998). *India: from midnight to millennium.* New York: HarperCollins.

Tylor, E. B. (1958). *Primitive culture.* New York: Harper.

Vohra, R. (2001). *The making of India.* (2nd. ed.) Armonk, NY: M.E. Sharpe.

Watson, F. (1975). *A concise history of India.* New York: Charles Scribner's Sons.

Wolpert, S. (1965). *India.* Englewood Cliffs, NJ: Prentice Hall, Inc.

Zaehner, R. (1966). The Atharva Veda, Brihadaranayka Upanishad, and The Rig Veda (Trans.). In *Hindu Scriptures.* London: J. M. Dent & Sons.

CHAPTER 4
The Garífuna Culture: A Proclaimed Masterpiece in Central America*
Francisca O. Norales

In March 2001, the United Nations Educational, Scientific, and Cultural Organization (UNESCO) for the first time awarded the title, "Masterpieces of the Oral and Intangible Heritage of Humanity" to 19 outstanding cultural forms of expression from different countries of the world. The criteria used in the selection process were outstanding value, roots in cultural tradition, affirmation of cultural identity, source of inspiration and intercultural exchange, contemporary cultural and social role, excellence in the application of skills, unique testimony of living cultural tradition, and risk of disappearing. It is hoped that proclamations will be made every two years by an international jury appointed by UNESCO.

According to Gallagher (2001), the Garífuna culture was selected because of the vibrancy of its language, music, and dance. However, the survival of this culture is at risk due to discriminatory land measures, the failure of local school systems to acknowledge the language and culture, and lack of government and financial support.

This research is based on the philosophical position that if one of the purposes of schooling is to assist students in the development of the whole being, human rights and responsibilities must become essential considerations as new courses are identified. In addition, activities as well as other educational experiences must be planned. Consequently, students will be assisted as they explore and classify their feelings and beliefs about themselves, their race, and ethnic group. Ultimately, students will learn how to relate and interact with individuals not only within their own ethnic group, but with other groups across society.

* This chapter originally appeared in Francisca O. Norales (2003), The Journal of Intergroup Relations, Vol. XXX, No. 2, pp 35–46, and is reprinted with permission.

Specifically, this article identifies those aspects of the Garífuna culture that contributed to being awarded with the title, "Masterpiece of the Oral and Intangible Heritage of Humanity." It is hoped that it will provide encouragement to educators and decision makers as they seek to identify ways of enhancing culturally diverse training strategies in the schools, including the teacher preparation programs.

This line of research forms the basis for developing a model curriculum and provides insights into incorporating a multicultural education component, which is sound, reasonable, and viable in serving the needs of a multi-ethnic society.

A Description of Belize

Belize, one of the Central American countries in which Garífuna is spoken, was one of 19 countries to receive the outstanding title, "Masterpiece of the Oral and Intangible Heritage of Humanity." Belize, formerly known as British Honduras, has been an independent nation since 1981. Located on the eastern coast of Central America, it shares borders on the north and northwest with Mexico, on the west and south with Guatemala, and is washed along the entire eastern coast by the Caribbean Sea. Belize is larger than El Salvador, its Central American neighbor, about twice the size of Jamaica, and about four times the size of Trinidad and Tobago. At its longest point, the country extends approximately 174 miles and is 68 miles across at its widest point. Belize's principal export commodities are unrefined sugar and molasses, citrus fruit segments, juices and concentrates, citrus oils, timber (such as mahogany and cedar), fish products (particularly lobsters, conch and scale fish) and garments (Belize Information Service Publication, 1995). Belize has a land area of 8,866 square miles including 266 square miles of coastal islands.

In keeping with the historical pattern of British colonialism, Belize has patterned its economic, legal, and education systems after those of Britain. One very important legacy of the British rule is the high value Belizeans place on education. With all its socio-economic changes, this developing nation has a literacy rate of 93 percent (Belize Information Service Publication, 1995). Belize's population consists of approximately

205, 000 multi-ethnic people: Garífuna, Creoles, Maya Indians, Mestizos, East Indians, Europeans, and Asians.

A Brief History of the Garífuna Culture

According to Crawford (1984), the Garífuna-speaking People of Belize form a biological and cultural amalgam of Arawak and Carib Indians with West African slaves. Taylor (1951) states that the African component was added to the original Amerindian population of St. Vincent from 1517 to 1646 in the form of runaway slaves from the European-held islands. He further states that there they adopted the language spoken in St. Vincent, and to a considerable extent, the culture. Between 1661 and 1668, St. Vincent was described as having all Indians and some Negroes from the loss of two Spanish ships in 1635.

Gonzalez (1969) states that by 1796, the Black Caribs were completely defeated by the English and were forced to surrender unconditionally. The English, fearful of the demonstrated power of some 5,000 Caribs, removed them from the island of St. Vincent. Therefore, in 1797 the Black Caribs were landed on the island of Roátan. They did not remain long in Roátan, but at the invitation of the Spanish Governor spread along the coast east and west of Trujillo, Honduras. Many got involved in the wars between the royalist and republican forces. When the royalist forces eventually lost, some of the Caribs who had served with them were forced to flee to other Central American countries. By 1802, the Garífuna-speaking people, Garínagu, were settled in Dangriga, and in the Toledo district of Belize, Central America.

Formal Education within the Garífuna Culture

The field of education was an area in which the churches and the missionaries in Belize performed their most important work. This area also aroused the deepest suspicion by the slave-owners throughout the West Indies. Just as the 19th century English factory owners saw no need for their employees to learn to read, so the sugar planters feared the effects of education on their slaves (Dobson, 1979). The wood cutters in Honduras seem more enlightened in that even though little was done to encourage it, they did not prevent the education of their slaves. In 1807, a free school for 10 poor children was established. By 1833, there were 90 to 120 boys attending school, while the Superintendent's wife held classes for girls (Dobson, 1979). While the Methodists were successful in setting up schools and establishing their mission stations outside Belize, they enjoyed considerable success among the Garífuna-speaking people in Dangriga. In 1834, the people built both a chapel and a school. In 1838, there were a total of 50 Garífuna-speaking students who were regularly attending school. Ten years later, the Methodists had four chapels for 400 church members and five teachers.

The Struggles of the Garífuna-Speaking People
In providing the first written account of the Garífuna-speaking people in their new homes, Young (1842) characterized them as peaceable, friendly, ingenious, industrious, and immoderately fond of dress. They were very anxious to have a school, and there was a strong desire for improvement among them.

> They are scrupulously clean, and have great aptitude for the acquirement of languages. Most of the men being able to talk in Carib, Spanish, and English; some even add Creole-French; I have heard even the women converse in Carib, Spanish, and French, or in Carib, English, and Spanish. (Young, 1842, p. 123)

Norales (1967) states that Garífuna are intelligent, have contributed to the high literacy rate in Belize, and have served with distinction in the primary schools in different racial communities in rural Belize. Their quick ability to learn the language of other ethnic groups is an asset, and have been influential in removing barriers, thereby encouraging open communication among other ethnic groups like the Mayas and Kekchies. In addition to Garífuna, many Garínagu speak Maya, Kikchi, Spanish and Creole. Of the two African descendants in Belize, Garínagu are the only ethnic group who possess distinctive language.

The struggles of the Garífuna-speaking people even prior to their arrival in Central America were not easy. Crawford (1984) states that their status should be viewed in national and historical perspectives. Burdon (1931) states that the Garífuna-speaking people "had to have a permit from the Superintendent" (p. 11) before they could be allowed in Dangriga. Sanford (1975) suggested that the prejudice stems from the status-consciousness of Creoles at that time, who were trying to cast off their black ancestry and the social disability it entailed, and to whom the Garífuna represented the epitome of what they despised in themselves. Palacio (1975) reported that wage labor was reinforced by the deliberate policy of not granting freehold ownership titles to Garínagu, but rather leasing them even though they had been occupying the land for cultivation of subsistence crops. Shoman (1994) states that in the middle of the 19th century, a large proportion of Belize's population was African, and by the end of the century, Belize had become an extremely racist society. Hyde (1975) states that discrimination on the basis of the color of one's skin persisted even after slavery was abolished. This has been perceived as a product of colonialism, which fostered discrimination. The color of one's skin does matter in the Belizean society and can be observed in the preferential treatment given to a Mestizo over a Garífuna or a Creole-speaking Belizean in hiring practices, politics, schools, and other areas.

Curriculum Planning: The Lingering Question
The United Nations Educational, Scientific, and Cultural Organization (UNESCO) has declared to the world including the Belizean society that it has an Afro-rich language and culture. From a broader consideration, culture is the driving force in a curriculum. Additionally, when a nation should respond to the following question, "What knowledge is worth the most?" that nation is confronted with basic civil rights and responsibilities. Unquestionably, human rights and responsibilities are considerations based on philosophical views that are grounded in values perceived as necessary to promulgate cultural legacy. Such legacy must be seen in the context of its importance to the cultivation of the young, those individuals who must carry with them what is presented in school. Regardless of its various forms and functions, culture performs those basic responsibilities through the process of schooling so that objectives can be achieved. The inclusion

of Garífuna language and culture into the Belizean curriculum requires the support of educators, decision makers, and the government.

How decision makers conceptualize curriculum affects roles for handling major issues. Additionally, curriculum allows decision makers to grow, learn, and to revise plans about schools and schooling. Curriculum is the heart of every school's program and is the most cogent concern of a culture's philosophy of education. Consequently, curriculum is a public issue. Since the public uses the results of curricular processes, public policy cannot be avoided, particularly when questions such as the following are asked: (1) What courses are being taught? (2) How well are the courses taught? and (3) What are the courses to be deleted, modified, or adopted? It follows that any approach to curricular design cannot be haphazard, but must be systematic and well planned.

Developing a Multicultural Curriculum

Teachers involved in the development of multicultural programs have to consider the accepted components of curriculum design such as needs assessment, goals and learning outcomes, implementation, teaching strategies, and evaluation.

To integrate multicultural perspectives into an existing curriculum, educators need to examine various facets of the existing program. This examination should include an initial assessment of student knowledge, attitudes, and skills and an evaluation of the curriculum as a whole. Doing otherwise can result in programs that are less sensitive to variations in student population, school environment, and community setting (Norales, 1996).

Although assessment of knowledge and skills is an accepted part of teaching, assessment of attitudes and perceptions is much less common. Many of the goals and objectives in multicultural education involve efforts to examine and even change how students see themselves, how they are viewed by others and how they view others.

Multicultural education advocates argue that the curriculum should be reformed so that it regularly presents diverse perspectives, experiences, and contributions, particularly those that tend to be omitted or misrepresented (Norales, 1996). Concepts should be selected and taught to represent diverse cultural groups and both genders. For example, if poetry is being taught, the teacher should select poetry written by members of a variety of groups. This teaches students that other groups have also written poetry and it also enriches the concept of poetry because it enables students to explore various poetic forms (Sleeter and Grant, 1988). Furthermore, it is recommended that the contributions a teacher selects represent each group as the group would represent itself and show the group as active and dynamic. This requires the teacher to learn about various groups and become sensitive to aspects of each group's culture that are important to that group. A related recommendation is that curricular materials and all visual displays be free of race, gender, and handicap stereotypes and include members of all groups in a positive manner.

In developing a multicultural curriculum in Belize, emphasis has to be placed on developing guidelines that will incorporate the following: (1) take seriously the composition of the ethnic group within each district, (2) focus on the needs of the teachers and students, (3) make equity a primary issue in education, and (4) embrace a framework that incorporates local and nation-wide concerns.

Language and Culture
The term "culture" may be defined in many ways, but anthropologists agree that the word refers to the complex processes of human social interaction and symbolic communication. It is a dynamic, creative, and a continuous process that includes behaviors, values, and substance learned and shared by people that guides them in their struggle for survival and gives meaning to their lives (Hernandez, 1989).

Language is the key to the heart of a culture. So related are language and culture that language holds the power to maintain national or cultural identity. According to Edwards (1985), language is important in ethnic and nationalist sentiment because of its power and visible symbolism; it becomes a core symbol or rallying point. The impact of Garífuna as a strong symbol of national identity is visible in that since the inception of schools in 1807, Garífuna was never included in the curriculum. Later, when secondary education evolved, while Spanish in addition to English were mandatory subjects, Garífuna as a required or elected subject was not, and continues not to be seen in the curriculum. Yet, when a youth returned home from school, the language chosen to converse in between parent and child or child and grandparent was Garífuna.

Because of the relationship between language and cultural identity, steps are often taken to prohibit the influence of other languages. For example, Costa Rica has enacted a law that restricts the use of foreign languages and imposes fines on those who break it. Under the law, companies that advertise in a foreign language must also include a Spanish translation in larger letters. Turkey's government is considering fining anyone who uses foreign names on the airwaves. Likewise, France has a list of 3,500 foreign words that cannot be used in school, bureaucracies, or companies (Samovar & Porter, 2001).

Verbal Processes

Clearly, it is impossible to separate language from culture. According to Rubin (1992), language is a set of characters or elements and rules for their use in relation to one another. These characters or elements are symbols, the words that are culturally diverse, and they differ from one culture to another. It can be discovered when studying another language that not only are the symbols (words) and sounds for those words different, but so are the rules (phonology, grammar, syntax, and intonation) for using those symbols and sounds.

Word differences are obvious in various languages. In English, one lives in a house. In Garífuna, one lives in a *muna*. Grammatical structures are unique to each language as well. In English, there are both singular and plural nouns and pronouns. In Garífuna, in addition to having singular and plural nouns and pronouns, a distinction is made by the context of the sentence and the gender of the speaker. Syntax, or the word order and structure of sentences, also varies depending on the language. In the normal order for simple sentences in Garífuna, the predicate is preceded by the subject. For example, the English sentence "The girl is ill" would be "*Sanditu erahe*" or "Sick girl" in Garífuna. These examples would indicate that if a person is to communicate in Garífuna, not only the symbols (words) of Garífuna should be known, but also the rules for using those symbols.

Language is much more than just a symbol and rule system that permits communication with another person; it is also the means by which people think and construct reality. According to Nanda and Warms (1998), language does more than just reflect culture; it is the way in which an individual is introduced to the order of the physical and social environment. In addition to Belize, Garífuna is spoken in other Central American countries such as Honduras, Guatemala, and Nicaragua. The arrival of Garínagu in Belize, which is celebrated annually on November 19 as Garífuna Settlement Day, is a national holiday in Belize.

Existing within decision makers is an attempt to reverse the goals and principles of multicultural inclusion in standard curricular procedures. Such efforts are given attention for a one-day celebration, thereby reducing the quest for inclusion to a single day. After that celebration, everything goes back to normal until the following year. Certainly, this is not good curriculum practice. Belizeans should not be content with piecemeal celebrations nor mini programs that are located at the periphery of the curriculum. Instead, efforts must be toward comprehensive, substantive programs that are intellectually and psychologically stimulating to reinforce ethnic identity and unity. It is because of their distinctiveness that Taylor (1951) described Garínagu as having a rich and remarkable culture. Additionally, their music and dance have been known to be creative, outstanding, and vibrant; hence one of the reasons for receiving the title, "Masterpiece of the Oral and Intangible Heritage of Humanity," and one of 19 outstanding cultural spaces or forms of expression as awarded by UNESCO.

The African Diaspora and Garífuna Music and Dance

Maultsby (1990) observed that among students of African-related culture in the Black diaspora, some cultural nuances die hard. Despite the institution of slavery and its negative effects, calculated efforts did not destroy the cultural legacy of the enslaved, nor diminish the memories of the African past. The survival of the enslaved in the New World depended on their ability to retain the fundamentals of African culture.

Although slaves were exposed to European-derived traditions, they resisted cultural imprisonment and retained their African past. They survived oppression through creativity, application of critical thinking-skills, and brought relevance to European customs by reshaping them to conform to African aesthetic ideals. The Garífuna culture, music, and dance are legacies of Africa in the Black diaspora.

Singing is an integral part of the Garífuna culture. The songs are many and consist of various types ranging from those sung during church services, cultural religious ceremonies, semi-sacred songs, and secular Garífuna songs. The sole instrument used during cultural religious ceremonies is the drum. In describing his observation during a cultural religious ceremony, Young (1842) indicated that he saw women in great numbers, joining in with the festivities.

> It was pleasing to observe their particularly modest and quiet behavior. They dance and sing, the dancing being merely a movement to and fro with their hands and feet, alternately, accompanied by a peculiar intonation of voice. (Young, 1842, p. 133)

The cultural religious ceremony, *dugú*, is an African-Indian ritual that is practiced in all Garífuna settlements. It is a time when families and extended families unite to celebrate and participate in their cultural rituals.

Abaimahani, a type of dance, is also a semi-sacred gestured song. The dancers who are generally females, can number as few as five to as many as thirty standing in line, and clasping each other by the thumb. As they sing, they swing their arms and bodies rhythmically; they flex their knees, while bending slightly forward, now to the left, and now to the right hand. Should a large number of women wish to participate, two rows are formed, and they face each other from a short distance.

Since music among the Garífuna-speaking people is included in almost all activities, it is not unusual to hear the sound of drums by the local drummers throughout the day. This is particularly so during the Christmas holidays when Garínagu in the southern districts are likely to celebrate the festive season by dancing to the beat of the drums through the major streets.

Because the Garífuna-speaking people are creative, several types of songs are known and sung. New songs keep evolving, and can be heard via the local radio stations. Today, many songs are available in the form of records, audio and videocassette tapes, and compact disks.

Drum rhythms are always produced with the hands alone, and are, during the *dugú* and *malí*, synchronic although polyrhythms are known, and are employed in some secular dances, such as *punta*. During the *dugú* dancing itself, a steady and monotonous rhythm consisting of one heavy and five light beats is kept up while during the *malí*, this changes to a quicker, one heavy and three light beats (Taylor, 1951). Dancers can be observed progressing energetically in concentric rings while they are singing.

Existing within the Garífuna-speaking people are the many types of dancing styles suitable for any occasion. A favorite, *Wanaragua*, also called John Canoe, is performed during the Christmas holidays. The male dancers, dressed in colorful and attractive head covers, wear a painted mask constructed from metal screen to cover their face. The dancers, dressed in white or in black pants or white jackets, can either wear a black or pink ribbon affixed to their attire. As they dance energetically to the beat of the drums, the movements from their feet and the rattling of the seashells tied to each knee all sound harmoniously to the beat of the drummers. The singing to accompany the drummers is performed by both women and men.

Wanaragua, an enjoyable dance within the Garífuna culture, has many male Garínagu living abroad return to the southern districts during the Christmas holidays to participate in the dance. The females, on the other hand, participate by singing along to accompany the drummers and the dancers while they perform.

Another of the many dances within the Garífuna-speaking culture is *Gunjai*. This dance, which is performed during special occasions and in formal settings, allows one to observe the grace exhibited by dancers and the quality of their movement to the beat of the drums. As dancers perform, each male has a female partner yet dances with all the females. Their movements are always graceful, unique, and attractive.

A very popular dance, *punta*, is danced during cultural religious ceremonies, Christmas holidays, and social gatherings. As couples dance to the beat of the drums, the steps are minute so that progress in any direction is extremely slow. Today, a variation of *punta*, which is called *punta rock*, has gained national recognition throughout Central America and the Caribbean.

CONCLUSION

Multicultural inclusion and human rights considerations must become a reality in the schools in Belize. Multicultural education affirms that schools should be oriented toward cultural enrichment of all students by providing activities and programs that are rooted in the idea of preservation and extension of cultural alternatives. Clearly, because a viable curriculum encompasses all the experiences and activities in school, a curriculum must be comprehensive in scope and sequence. Incorporating the Garífuna language, music, and dance into the Belizean curriculum requires the attention, support, and encouragement of educators, the government, decision makers, and the media. An endangered or even an extinct language can be saved through a determined language policy.

REFERENCES

Belize Information Service Publication (1995). *Fact sheet: Belize*. Belmopan, Belize: The Government Printing Department.

Burden, J. (1931). *Archives of British Honduras*. London: Sifton Praed.

Crawford, M. (Ed.) (1984). *Black Caribs: A case study in biocultural adaptation* (Vol. 3). New York: Plenum Press.

Dobson, N. (1973). *A history of Belize*: Trinidad and Jamaica: LongmanCaribbean Ltd.

Edwards, J. (1985). *Language, society and identity* Oxford, UK: Blackwell.

Gallagher, N. (2001). *Did you know?* [On-line]. Retrieved September 7, 2001 from http://magma.nationalgeographic.com.

Gonzalez, N. (1969). *Black Carib household structure: A study of migration and modernization*. Seattle: University of Washington Press.

Hernandez, H. (1989). *Multicultural education: A teacher's guide to content and process*. New York: Macmillan Publishing Company.

Hyde, E. (1975). *Feelings: Colourism: The deeper problem*. Belize: Benex Press.

Maultsby, P. (1990). *Africanisms in African-American music*. In Holloway, J. (Ed.). *Africanisms in American culture*. Bloomington: Indiana University Press.

Nanda, S., & Warma, R. (1998). *Cultural anthropology*. Belmont, CA: Wadsworth/Thompson Learning Inc.

Norales, F. 0. (1996). Multicultural education. *Journal of Caribbean Studies, 11*,154161.

Norales, F. S. (1967). *The Joint Role of the Adolescent and Adult in Community Development*. Dissertation for the Post Graduate Diploma in Home Economics Related to Community Development. London: University of London.

Palacio, J. (1975.). *Problems in the maintenance of the Garífuna (Black Carib) culture in Belize*. Paper presented at the American Anthropological Association, San Francisco.

Rubin, B. (1992). *Communicating and human behavior*. Englewood Cliffs, NJ: Prentice Hall.

Sanford, M. (1975). *From the bottom looking up in a developing country*. Paper presented at the American Anthropological Association, San Francisco.

Samovar, L., & Porter, R. (2001). *Communication between cultures*. Belmont, CA: Wadsworth/Thompson Learning Inc.

Shoman, A. (1994). *Thirteen chapters of a history of Belize*. Belize City, Belize: The Angelus Press Ltd.

Sleeter, C., & Grant, C. (1988). *Making choices for multicultural education: Five approaches to race, class, and gender*. New York; Macmillan Publishing Company.

Taylor, D. (1951). *The Black Carib of British Honduras* (No. 17). New York: Viking Fund Publications.

United Nations Educational, Scientific, and Cultural Organization (UNESCO). (2001). *Proclamation of Masterpieces of the Oral and Intangible Heritage of Humanity*. [Online], Retrieved November 12, 2002 from http://www.unesco.org/bpi/intangible_heritage/

Young, T. (1842). *Narrative of a residence on the Mosquito Shore during the years 1839–1841*. London: Blackwell Publishers.

CHAPTER 5
Multiculturalism in Canada
Francisca O. Norales and Geraldine M. Norales

The word "multiculturalism" emerged in Canada during the 1960s to counter the word "biculturalism". The term was used by the Royal Commission on Bilingualism and Biculturalism, and it quickly became popular among professionals. In 1971, the federal government proclaimed a policy of multiculturalism within a bilingual, that is, an English and French framework. Around the same time, several provinces also proclaimed policies of multiculturalism. This essay explores the multiculturalism concept within the Canadian context, and examines the status of the African-Canadian in the workforce of Canada.

THE CANADIAN SOCIETY
The Canadian Society has always been ethnically, culturally and linguistically diverse, but in the twentieth century, the diversity had increased greatly. It was from 1896–1905 that the Minister of the Interior inaugurated a vigorous immigration campaign that resulted in three million people entering the country (Burnet, 1988).

Of the three million who entered the country, approximately one and a quarter million were from the British Isles, a million from the United States, and the remainder from continental Europe, and east and south Asia. Germans, Dutch, Scandinavians, Ukrainians, Poles, Hungarians, Russians, Italians, Jews, Chinese, Japanese and South Asians arrived (Ibid). They inhabited the prairie west, the construction, mining, and lumbering camps of the north and west coast, and the cities of Ontario and Quebec. After World War I, another wave of immigration began, which lasted until the depression of the 1930s, which brought in a million and a quarter immigrants (Ibid).

After World War II, a third wave arrived largely from traditional sources until 1967. Since then, immigrants from the various continents have arrived. The proportion of the population not of British, French or

First Nations (native people) origin increased from 8% in 1871 to 10% in 1901, and approximately 25% in 1971 (Ibid., p. 2).

Ethnic Diversity

Ethnic diversity including the composition of groups varies from region to region. The oldest parts of the country, the four Atlantic Provinces, have the lowest proportion of people of origins other than British, French, Indian, and Inuit. Quebec, where the majority and the politically and socially dominant group is French Canadian, has substantial British, Jewish, and Italian groups. Other groups such as Haitians emerged as a result of immigration.

Ontario, once largely British, French Canadian, and German, received approximately half of the Post-World War II immigration. One-third of its population is of other ethnic origins including a substantial portion of foreign birth. The three prairie provinces of Manitoba, Saskatchewan, and Alberta were settled during the massive wave of immigration before World War I, and have the greatest proportion of the population belonging to other ethnic origin (Ibid.).

According to Burnet (1988), only the province of Alberta drew many immigrants after World War II but was losing them because of depressed conditions. Although Ontario has begun to rival it, British Columbia had a substantial Scandinavian population.

However, because of its location on the Pacific, British Columbia had more people of Asian origin than any other region.

Unlike the United States that is often described as a melting pot, Canada has long taken pride in being a Mosaic of different cultures and ethnic groups. The dominant British group assumed that the immigrants admitted including their descendants should assimilate to the British group. The ease of admission was related to the presumed ability to assimilate. Consequently, northern Europeans were welcomed; eastern, central, and southern Europeans were let in grudgingly; while Asians and Africans were harshly restricted, if not, excluded (Ibid. p. 2).

In the 1960s when there was heightened concern on human rights and the emergence of ethnicity as a dominant theme throughout the world, other ethnic groups showed new assertiveness, along with an awakening of ethnic consciousness. Being aware of their numerical strength, their spokespersons attempted to create a "Third Force" to play a mediating role between English and French Canadians. This idea, lead by the Ukrainian Canadians, estimated the strength of the Third Force as being equal to those listed in the census of non-British and non-French origins, which consisted of one-third of the population.

John Porter, a sociologist, was at the same time insisting that ethnic and cultural differences should be ignored in the interest of equality. To Porter, the Mosaic was viewed as a division of labor by which the British maintained a privileged position and relegated all others to inferior status (Burnet, 1988).

A further result of the multicultural movement in the 1960s was the removal of formal discrimination on the basis of race or ethnicity from immigration regulations.

The change in regulations led to a vast increase of non-white immigrants from the West Indies and Asia. However, the policy of multiculturalism and the popular pride in ethnic diversity as a characteristic of Canadian society did not prevent racist outbursts.

Hate Crime Incidents

For the first time in 1999, the General Social Survey (GSS) on criminal victimization included measures to assess the nature and extent of hate crime in Canada.

The objectives of the survey were as follows: 1) to provide estimates of the prevalence of eight types of hate crimes; 2) to examine the wide array of related factors and characteristics of the incidents as well as the victims involved; and 3) to address current and emerging social issues since hate crime had been identified as a priority policy issue. The eight types of hate crimes were as follows: gender, religion, age, culture, race / ethnicity, sexual orientation, disability, and language.

Based on the findings from the General Social Survey (GSS), 43% of hate crimes were motivated by race. The findings of the study also revealed that 92% hate crime victims lived in urban areas. A broader regional breakdown further revealed that British Columbia had the highest rate of personal hate crime victimization per 1,000 population aged 15 years and older (Statistics Canada, Catalogue No. 85–551, 2001).

THE CANADIAN MULTICULTURALISM POLICY

Although there appears to be no agreement on the precise meaning of multiculturalism in Canada, it has connotations of a public policy, an ideology, and cultural diversity. According to Li (1999), many Canadians might have difficulty defining multiculturalism clearly, and yet, when asked in opinion polls, most Canadians have something to say about the concept. The uncertainty of the term has to do with its many facets in the Canadian context (Kallen, 1982). The conceptual ambiguity has also produced what Moodley (1983) called "the confusion of myth and reality" of the Canadian multiculturalism policy.

Advocates of multiculturalism in Canada use the term as a democratic value to promote equality, to combat racial and cultural discrimination, and to lobby for collective rights of minorities (Li, 1999, p. 150). Defining multiculturalism as a democratic reality in which there are substantial ethnic diversities and cleavages, implies that a policy to deal with pluralism impacts and can harmonize race and ethnic relations.

According to Li (1999), the federal policy provided only moderate financial assistance to ethnic groups to pursue their cultural expressions. The government also chose to create separate programs under direct government administration to promote minority arts, cultures, and heritages that became subsumed under multiculturalism. Similarly, multiculturalism did not transform Canadian institutions in the same way as official bilingualism. Instead, the multiculturalism policy was to support what Fleras & Elliott (1992) declared "a restructuring of the symbolic order to incorporate all identities on an equal basis," or what others characterized as token or symbolic pluralism. (Brotz ,1980; Roberts & Clifton, 1982).

In the 1980s, the federal government became more sensitive to issues of racial equality as immigration trends altered the racial composition of the Canadian population. This, in turn, created new expectations among minorities for the multiculturalism policy.

The 1980s witnessed expanded immigration from Third World

countries, and the concentration of immigrants in metropolitan areas such as Toronto, Vancouver, and Montreal (Li, 1999). Similarly, immigrants from the United States and the United Kingdom accounted for 20% of the 143,287 immigrants who were admitted. Additionally, in 1988, immigrants from the U.S. and the U.K. consisted of 10% of the total immigration. In contrast, immigrants from Asia, Pacific Islands, Africa, and the Middle East consisted of 57% of all the immigrants admitted that year (Canada, Employment and Immigration 1989).

Increased immigration from Third World countries throughout the 1980s added to the number of "visible minorities" in Canada. According to the 1981 census, 894,210 or 4% of the Canadian population belonged to origins from countries such as Africa, Asia, and Latin America (Statistics Canada,1984). In 1991, Canadians of African, African-Caribbean, Asian, Central and South American origin, accounted for 7.6% of Canada's population (Statistics Canada, 1993). The 1996 census indicated a further increase in visible minority population to 3.2 million people, or 22.2% of Canada's population. (Statistics Canada, 1998).

The Definition of Visible Minority
In addressing the effects of systemic discrimination, the Royal Commission on Equality in Employment recommended that the government of Canada pass legislation to accomplish the following: 1) make employment equity mandatory for employers in the public and private sectors; 2) provide effective arrangements to monitor compliance; 3) impose sanctions for failure to demonstrate efforts; and 4) attain employment equity goals. As a result, the government in response introduced the Employment Equity Act of 1986.

Within the context of the Employment Equity Act, visible minorities were defined as "persons other than an Aboriginal who are non-Caucasian in race or non-white in color and who so identify themselves to an employer or agree to be so identified by an employee" (Employment and Immigration Canada, 1989, p. 25).

Under the Employment Equity Act of 1986, federally regulated businesses were required to submit annual reports indicating their employment profiles regarding four target groups which are as follows:

1) visible minorities; 2) Aboriginal peoples; 3) women and 4) persons with disabilities. The categories for visible minority groups are as follows: Black, Chinese, Japanese, Korean, Filipino, Indo-Pakistani, West Asia and Arab, Southeast Asian, Latin American, Indonesian, and Pacific Islander. (Employment and Immigration Canada, 1986).

THE WORKFORCE OF CANADA

According to Satzewich (1999), until the 1950s, there was a clear and explicit sense in which employers in Canada saw different groups as possessing different social abilities and capacities. These differences were seen in biological or cultural terms, and used ideas about different group capabilities as a rationale for allocating them to different kinds of jobs. Canadian immigration was characterized by a racialized hierarchy, which was important in determining the groups to be excluded from the possibility of entering Canada, and in assigning groups to certain kinds of jobs and social positions.

Employment Equity

In the 1960s, Canada's immigration policy brought an increased number of people from the Third World. Appproximately one-half settled in Toronto, Ontario. According to Samuel & Karam (2000), the Canadian public was unprepared to cope with such large numbers of visible minority immigrants in their midst. While social tensions arose, 1977 was an important year for race relations and the resulting violence against South Asians in Toronto. When evidence based on studies in the U.S. showed that the affirmative action programs were effective in increasing the employment and earnings of minorities, employment equity programs in Canada received a positive boost.

Several research studies (Samuel, 1984; Billingsley & Musynski, 1985; Basavarajappa et al., 1993) indicated that persons with origins in the Third World experienced higher rates of unemployment, had lower salaries, and were unable to find work in their chosen fields. In addition, among graduates from Canadian universities and colleges, the employment rates of visible minorities were substantially lower than those of other graduates by approximately 8% for university graduates and 6% for community college graduates. These differences, which were attributed to lower participation rates and higher unemployment rates for visible minority graduates, appeared for graduates in almost all fields of study in most regions, except British Columbia (Wannel & Caron, 1994).

Diversity in the Banking Sector
According to Driedger & Halli (2000), the federally regulated employers in the private sector with the banks leading, did much better in hiring visible minorities at a time when the total numbers of employees were declining. This can indicate that declining overall employment is not necessarily a reason to curtail the employment of visible minorities. According to the Annual Report of The Canadian Human Rights Commission (1988), there was a higher representation of women in banks. Although many were employed as clerical workers, both genders increased their share of jobs in the middle managerial, professional and supervisory occupational levels.

When the employment practices for visible minorities were rank ordered, the Bank of Montreal was found to be the best in overall employment practices for visible minorities. The National Bank was ranked as the worst (Poole, 1989).

The largest of the chartered banks, the Royal Bank, was active in accessing and recruiting candidates including visible minorities. The approaches used were as follows: 1) making employment equity a priority for senior management; 2) outreach initiatives; 3) setting aside training or summer positions for visible minorities; 4) encouraging the staff to take active roles in visible minority organizations; 5) funding upgrading costs of employees; and 6) cross-cultural awareness training programs for senior and line managers (Driedger & Halli, 2000).

ECONOMIC CONTRIBUTIONS OF THE AFRICAN-CANADIAN

Economists use the term "human capital" to imply the accumulated education and training workers receive that increase their productivity

(Taylor & Johnson, 1997). According to this theory, the more educated job seekers are, the more likely they are to obtain well-paying and higher-status jobs, and the less likely they are to be unemployed than their less-educated counterparts. The theory assumes that the economic contributions that different jobs make to society determine the respective remuneration in the workforce. Unfortunately, some of the minority groups including the African-Canadian do not benefit as they should from their human capital in the Canadian labor market due to the prevalence of racial exploitation in the workforce (Mensah, 2002).

The Vertical Mosaic Thesis

In 1965, the Carleton University sociologist, John Porter, initiated a period of intense academic discourse on ethnic and racial stratification in Canada. The empirical data, which was derived from the 1931, 1951, and 1961 censuses, centered on claims that ethnic and racial affiliations were critical determinants of occupational roles, and consequently, class formation. Awareness grew that Canada is not a classless society with non-existing perceptible income and occupational lines across racial and ethnic groups. Similarly, it was noted that Porter's vertical mosaic was not a scientific theory with a universal application, but a thesis consisting of several loosely connected suppositions about the nature of ethnic stratification in Canadian society (Ibid).

According to Porter (1965), people of white Anglo-Saxon Protestant ancestry prevailed in the top of Canadian vertical mosaic, while Aboriginal people occupied the bottom. Although there was a small percentage of African descendants in Canada, Porter said very little about them, and viewed them as non-entities within Canadian society (Ibid.).

Porter's thesis was disputed, appraised, and subjected to different interpretations. Darrouch (1979) found that while the rank-order of ethnic groups had been stable, ethnic occupational dissimilarity as measured by the index of dissimilarity, decreased between 1931 and 1971. Consequently, it was concluded that ethnicity was far less important in stratifying the Canadian workforce than Porter had asserted.

The Workforce of Canada

By using the 1931, 1951, 1961, and 1971 census data, Lautard & Loree (1984) found that although ethnic inequality in the job market was decreasing, Porter's vertical mosaic "remains a durable feature of Canadian society." Furthermore, the findings indicated that ethnic inequalities in occupations to be four times greater than gender inequalities. This can confirm the persistence of Porter's vertical mosaic in Canadian society.

The data in Table 1 indicate the percentage of workers by employment equity groups for "Blacks," "all visible minorities," and "all Canadians" since 1995.

Table 1

Total Population 15 Years of Age and Over Who Worked Since January 1, 1995, by Employment Equity Groups for Blacks, All Visible Minorities, and All Canadians

Occupation	Blacks N=269,065 (%)	All Visible Minorities N=1,593,635 (%)	All Canadians N=15,547,120 (%)
Senior managers	0.27	0.69	0.97
Middle and other managers	3.81	7.04	7.67
Professionals	12.71	14.14	13.92
Semi-professionals/technicians	6.06	5.42	6.13
Supervisors	1.28	1.16	1.21
Supervisor: Crafts and trades	1.10	1.22	3.48
Administrative and senior clerical	3.43	3.85	5.41
Skilled sales and services	4.14	5.48	4.59
Skilled crafts and trades	5.45	4.92	7.45
Clerical personnel	14.52	12.52	11.07
Intermediate sales and service	13.84	12.68	12.33
Semi- skilled manual workers	13.80	13.33	11.48
Other sales and service personnel	14.45	13.04	10.16
Other manual workers	5.03	4.45	4.06

Source: Canada, Statistics Canada 1999b.

The data in Table 1 indicate that while the percentage of "all Canadians" in the senior managerial level was 0.97 %, the percentage for "Blacks" was 0.27%. Clearly, there is an under-representation of "Blacks" in managerial positions in Canada.

The data in Table 1 further indicate that the proportion of "Blacks" in middle and other managerial positions to be small in comparison to the percentage for "all visible minorities," and "all Canadians." Other observed findings indicate a higher percentage of "Blacks" to be found in the lower occupational positions such as clerical personnel, intermediate sales and service, semi- skilled manual workers, and other sales and service personnel.

The data in Table 2 provide the labor market indicators for "Blacks" by provinces or territories in 1996.

Table 2
The Labor Market Indicators for Blacks by Provinces or Territories in 1996.

Province/ Territory	Unemployment Rate		University Education		Average Income	
	Blacks	Prov./Terr.	Blacks	Prov./Terr.	Blacks	Prov./Terr.
	%	%	%	%	$	$
Newfoundland/ Labrador	32.6	25.1	44.15	18.78	16,526	19,710
P.E.I.	*	13.8	48.71	22.10	*	20,527
Nova Scotia	20.0	13.3	17.65	23.46	16,007	21,552
New Brunswick	19.9	15.5	21.43	20.08	18,039	20,755
Quebec	11.8	26.3	24.46	20.19	15,483	23,198
Ontario	18.3	9.1	20.11	24.32	20,144	27,309
Manitoba	10.4	7.9	33.03	23.11	19,931	22,667
Saskatchewan	11.2	7.2	36.39	21.61	21,331	22,541
Alberta	11.0	7.2	25.86	23.52	20,383	26,138
B.C.	16.0	9.6	29.82	25.48	21,310	26,295
Yukon	*	11.0	33.33	26.47	*	29,079
N.W.T.	6.9	12.9	39.39	18.08	*	29,011

* No data available   Source: Canada, Statistics Canada 1999b

The data in Table 2 indicate that while Ontario's unemployment rate for 1996 was 9.1 %, the unemployment percentage rate for "Blacks" was 18.3%. Similarly, in Newfoundland / Labrador, the provincial unemployment rate was 25.1%, while the unemployment percentage rate for Blacks was 32.6%. Clearly, the unemployment rate for "Blacks" is higher in all the Canadian provinces or territories.

Based on the data provided in Table 2, with the exception of Nova Scotia and Ontario, the "Black" population has a higher percentage of individuals with university education in all the provinces or territories.

According to the data provided in Table 2, disparities exist between the average income of "Blacks" and their non-Black counterparts in all provinces or territories. For example, while the average income in Ontario was $27,309, the average income for "Blacks" was $20,144.

Based on the data provided in Table 2, within the "Black" population of Canada, there is an under-representation in high-status occupations, higher unemployment rate in all provinces or territories, a higher percentage of workers with university education in most provinces or territories, and lower average annual incomes.

The African-Canadian Women and the Canadian Workforce

One of the trends in Canada since the early 1960s is the increasing number of women in the workplace (Ghalam, 1994; Hiller, 1991). Yet, Canadian women are still concentrated in traditional female jobs such as nursing, retail, clerical, and other business services, and still earn incomes that are lower than those of men (Preston & Giles, 1997; Hiller, 1991). While the existence of gender inequalities in the Canadian workforce is indisputable, Mensah (2002) noted that women experience life not only through the prism of gender, but also through that of race, ethnicity and class. Billson (1991) pointed out that race, like gender, carries the connotation of power in a society. Mensah (2002) pointed out that it is widely believed among members of the "Black" community that the "Black" Canadian-women, like their male counterparts, continue to encounter discrimination not only in nursing and domestic work, where many have traditionally gained employment, but in almost all levels of the economy. This is practiced despite the growing public awareness and acceptance of democratic ideals such as equal rights, justice, and the feminist movement on women's rights in Canada.

The data in Table 3 provide the educational, employment characteristics, and income indicators for "Black women," "all visible minority women," and "all Canadian women" in 1996.

Table 3

The Educational, Employment, and Income Indicators for Black Women, All Visible Minority Women, and All Canadian Women in 1996.

Variable	Black Women	All Visible Minority Women	All Canadian Women
Education and language Characteristics			
% with neither English nor French ability	1.70	11.19	1.97
With less than Grade 9 education	9.45	14.00	12.38
% with university education	19.9	29.90	22.28
Employment and Income Characteristics			
Labor force participation rate (%)	62.6	57.6	58.6
Unemployment rate (%)	19.8	15.3	10.0
% in senior management positions	0.19	0.29	0.44
% in middle and other management positions	3.05	4.87	5.55
Average full-time employment income	$27,561	$27,465	$30,130
Average part-time employment income	$12,461	$12,244	$12,727
Average annual income	$16,959	$16,621	$19,208
% of income from govt. transfer payment	22.1	15.9	11.8

Source: Canada, Statistics Canada 1999b.

According to the data in Table 3, a small difference, less than four percent exists between the percentage of "Black women" with education and language characteristics as compared to "all Canadian women." For example, while the percentage of "Black women" with neither English nor French ability was 1.70 %, the percentage for "all Canadian women" was 1.97 %. Similarly, while the percentage of "Black women" with university education was 19.9 %, the percentage for "all Canadian women" was 22.28 %.

Based on the data in Table 3, the percentage of "Black women" occupying senior and middle managerial positions is far less in comparison to "all Canadian women" and "all visible minority women."

Other observed findings from the data in Table 3 are that while the labor force participation rate was the highest (62.6 %) for "Black women" in comparison to "all Canadian women" (58.6 %), and "all visible minority women" (57.6 %), the unemployment rate among "Black women" was the highest, 19.8 % in comparison to 15.3 % for "all visible minority women," and 10.0 % for "all Canadian women."

While the average full-time and part-time employment income as well as the average annual income for "Black women" was slightly higher than that of "all visible minority women," the average full-time and part-time employment income and the average annual income for "all Canadian women" was the highest.

The data in Table 3 further reveal that in comparison to "all visible minority women," and "all Canadian women," "Black women" derive the highest percentage of their income from government transfer payment.

Although the average annual income of "Black women" is slightly higher than "all visible minority women," the average annual incomes for "Black women" and "all visible minority women," are lower than the average income of "all Canadian women."

According to Li (2002), gender and racial origin interact with immigrant status to produce complex interactive effects on earnings. Immigrant women of visible minority origin suffer the most income disadvantage in comparison to other immigrant groups, although immigrant women not of visible minority suffer only marginally less. These findings persisted in all census of the metropolitan area. Additional findings suggested that even though larger immigrant communities and lower unemployment rates in larger urban markets do increase the earnings of immigrant women, they remain at the bottom of the income hierarchy among all immigrant and native-born groups.

CONCLUSIONS

Although there have been many interpretations of the term "multiculturalism" in Canada, it is clear that the concept has gained legitimacy within Canadian society.

Many forces, primarily the Federal government's endorsement of multiculturalism as a desirable policy, have contributed to the process of legitimizing the multiculturalism debate. The official stand towards multiculturalism, the ideological promise of a multicultural society, and the quality programs supported by public funds have resulted in a new area where the politics of cultural diversity have been pursued.

As African-Canadians and visible minorities respond to the official policy of cultural diversity and the promise of multiculturalism, their actions become prompted by the official multiculturalism policy. Clearly, the official policy of multiculturalism provides not only a political legitimacy to multiculturalism, but also produces consequences that help reinforce the image of Canada as a society that is tolerant of its various ethnic diversities.

The status of the African-Canadian women would indicate that in the case of immigrants in the Canadian workforce, how well the African-Canadian women perform relative to native-born Canadian women is a function of how prepared the society is to reward the African-Canadian equitably, regardless of the perceived differences in gender and race.

Within the Canadian workforce barriers need to be removed so that the contributions of African-Canadians can be recognized and rewarded. This will result in a multicultural workforce that is inclusive, dynamic, and adaptive.

REFERENCES

Basavarajappa, K. Beaujot, R. & Samuel, T. (1993). *Impact of Immigration in the receiving countries.* Geneva: International Organization for Migration.

Billingsley, B. & Musynski, L. (1985). *No discrimination here.* Toronto: Social Planning Council of Metro Toronto and the Urban Alliance on Race Relations.

Billson, J. (1991). Interlocking identities: Gender, ethnicity and power in the Canadian context. *International journal of Canadian studies* 3, 49–67.

Brotz, H. (1980). Multiculturalism in Canada: A muddle. *Canadian Public Policy* 6, 41–46.

Burnet, J. (1988). *Multiculturalism in Canada*. Ottawa: Department of the Secretary of the State of Canada.

Canada, Employment and Immigration (1989). *Immigration to Canada: A statistical overview.* Ottawa: Public Affairs and the Immigration Policy Branch.

Canada, Statistics Canada 1999b. Dimension Series. Canadian Demographic Characteristics (Including Language and Mobility). 1996 Census. Cat. No. 94F0008XCB. Ottawa: Statistics Canada.

Canadian Human Rights Commission. (1989). Annual Report, 1988. Ottawa: Supply and Services Canada.

Darrouch, G. (1979). Another look at ethnicity, stratification and social mobility in Canada. *Canadian Journal of Sociology* 4, 1–25.

Driedger, L. & Halli, S. (2000). *Race and Racism: Canada's challenge.* Montreal: McGill-Queen's University Press.

Fleras, A. & Elliott, J. (1992). *Multiculturalism in Canada. The challenge of diversity.* Scarborough: Nelson Canada.

Ghalam, N. (1994). Women in the workplace. *Canadian Social Trends 2.* Toronto: Thompson Educational.

Hiller, H. (1991). *Canadian Society: A Micro Analysis.* Scarborough, ON: Prentice.

Kallen, E. (1982). Multiculturalism: Ideology, policy and reality. *Journal of Canadian Studies* 17, 51–63.

Lautard, H. & Loree, D. (1984). Ethnic stratification in Canada 1931–1971. *Canadian Journal of Sociology* 9, 334–343.

Li, P. (1999). *Race and ethnic relations in Canada.* Ontario: Oxford University Press.

Mensah, J. (2002). *Black Canadians: History, experiences, social conditions.* Halifax: Fernwood Publishing.

Moodley, R. (1983). Canadian multiculturalism as ideology. *Ethnic and Racial Studies* 6, 320–331.

Preston, V. & Giles, W. (1997). Ethnicity, gender and labour markets in Canada: A case study of immigrant women in Toronto. *Canadian Journal of Urban Research* 6 (2), 135–59.

Porter, J. (1965). *The vertical mosaic.* Toronto: University of Toronto Press.

Poole, P. (1989). *Minorities in banking.* Ottawa: The Canadian Centre for Policy Alternatives.

Roberts, L. & Clifton, R. (1982). Exploring the ideology of Canadian multiculturalism. *Canadian Public Policy* 8, 88–94.

Samuel, J. & Karam, A. Employment equity for visible minorities. In Driedger, L. & Halli, S. (Eds.) (2000). *Race and Racism: Canada's challenge.* Montreal: McGill-Queen's University Press.

Samuel, T. (1984). Economic adaptation of refugees in Canada: Experience of a quarter century. *International Migration* 22, 10–21.

Statistics Canada (1991). 1991 Census Dictionary. Catalogue no. 92–301E. Ottawa: Supply and Services Canada.

_____ (2001). Hate Crime in Canada: An Overview of Issues and Data Sources. Catalogue no. 85–551. Ottawa: Minister of Industry.

_____ (1999b). Dimension Series. Canadian Demographic Characteristics (Including Language and Mobility). 1996 Census. Cat. no. 94F0008XCB. Ottawa: Statistics Canada.

_____ (1998). The Daily, 17 February. Catalogue no. 11–001E. Ottawa: Supply and Services Canada.

Satzewich, V. Political economy of race and ethnicity. In Li, P. (Ed.). (1999) *Race & Ethnic Relations in Canada* (1999). Ontario: Oxford University Press.

Taylor, J. & Johnson, D. (1997). *Principles of macroeconomics.* Toronto: ITP Nelson.

Wannel, T. & Caron, N. (1994). A look at employment equity groups among recent postsecondary graduates: Visible Minorities. *Aboriginal Peoples and their activity limited.* Ottawa: Statistics Canada, Supply and Services Canada.

CHAPTER 6
Relationship-Building Between the Police and Inner-City African-American Minorities
Concetta C. Culliver

In the publication "Multicultural Law Enforcement," Shusta, Levine, Wong, and Harris (2005) wrote that many African-Americans continue to be impacted by the deep scars brought about by the institution of slavery. More notable among those from the lower socioeconomic classes, the authors lamented that with the continuous pain emanating from the psychological heritage of slavery coupled with ongoing racial discrimination, realizing the "American dream" will never occur for them. This essay will focus on the problems, issues, and concerns associated with African-American minorities in the inner-city, police multicultural relationships, and police communication methodology with African-American minorities.

INNER CITY AMERICA
Urban America, with its inner city regions structured around "Metropolitan Segregation" and heavily populated by African-American minorities lends itself to socioeconomic and class status, whereby one would observe higher rates of low-income African-American minorities residing within inner city neighborhoods, while middle to upper class African-American minorities maintain residences in the more affluent sections of metropolitan areas. Moreover, "Ghetto Regions" is how some criminologists and sociologists have categorized America's inner city areas (Blauner, 1972; Shelden, 2001; Tabb, 1970; Wadman & Allison, 2004). Such American inner-city areas are analogous to "imperialized colonies" (Blauner, 1972; Tabb, 1970) and almost always detached from mainstreamed society, literally and figuratively.

Interestingly, Blauner (1972) coined a five step framework to illustrate and describe how African American "Ghetto" residents are colonized. First, there is "forced involuntary entry." Second, policies that serve to constrain, transform, or destroy the culture of African-American citizens of these regions are executed by the colonizers. Third, those colonized have the experience of being managed and manipulated by outsiders who look down upon them with scorn and disdain. Fourth, racism is a key factor of social domination by which a group seen as inferior or different due to alleged biological characteristics is exploited, controlled, and oppressed socially and physically by a superordinate group. Finally, separation based on labor status occurs, with the colonized being assigned menial and unskilled employment or often relegated to the "surplus labor force."

This segment of Urban America (inner-city), when analyzed or characterized, depicts extreme poverty, high illiteracy, inadequate education, increased high school dropout rates, lack of vocational training skills, considerable family disintegration, more single-headed households (mainly maternal), high unemployment, high rates of illegal drug possession, considerable neighborhood deterioration and decay, high teen pregnancy rates, and high HIV infestation. In addition, the arrest, conviction, and incarceration rate for black males, including young black males, is extremely high. Also, on the increase can be found high arrest, conviction, and incarceration rates for the young black female juvenile offender. Heavy concentrations of high rate offenders predominate these areas.

CYCLICAL POVERTY IN METROPOLITAN GHETTO REGIONS

Caution should be extended when analyzing or pondering the conditions of those trapped in metropolitan ghetto regions. It is "cyclical poverty"; it is vicious, unbreakable, and intergenerational in nature. These residents are victims of societal ills; many are second and third generations of impoverished individuals; therefore, blaming them for their inability to escape the cycle of poverty or seeing them as worthless, irresponsible, and undeserving citizens is unrealistic. Furthermore, they reside in this type of environment simply because they cannot afford to live elsewhere.

Their neighborhoods are labeled in many ways as are so many perceptions and conclusions created about their residential living. For example, "disorganized" or "disorganization" are key concepts used to portray America's metropolitan ghetto areas, primarily because of the high reported crime rates and public sentiments that many inhabiting these areas are uncaring, irresponsible, and criminal. In fact, the majority of those residing in these areas are responsible citizens who are not fortunate to have an income beyond the poverty level. Many are domestic workers or maintain other menial low-skilled employment. Many report to work daily, expect protection from the police, pay their bills as far as their earnings will extend, and retain the same desires for their children as other parents. Their social values are no different, only the means of attaining those values because of the "anomic stress" stemming from "cyclical poverty." Of great importance is the need to equip inner-city children with consistent parental disciplinary guidelines; to instill in them the need to become good law-abiding citizens and to respect authority figures, including the police. At the same time, they realize that from America's Metropolitan ghetto lands have emerged many strong African-American leaders, male and female, known not only in the U.S. society but worldwide.

What is so alarming is the relationship between the police and African-American minorities. A strained relationship does exist. According to Purpura (2001), this strained-type relationship has existed down through the years. Even when African-American minorities strive to improve their civil rights and their social and economic conditions positively with governmental and private sector officials, still their actions are hampered when they encounter the police who serve as "gatekeepers" to government, representing what has been termed "the establishment." On May 1, 1992, when Rodney King, almost beaten to death by Los Angeles police, stepped to the microphone while most of South-Central Los Angeles was heavily engulfed in flames, he uttered in a halting voice, "Can't we all just get along?" Citizens, after hearing "the full acquittal verdict" of four Caucasian officers charged with excessive use of force against Rodney King, expressed their outrage over what they strongly believed to have been an unjust verdict. Yet, when King's words blasted across the airwaves, police officers nationwide scoffed and found it difficult to believe the man at the center of the turmoil engulfing Los Angeles would utter such remarks. But King was far from wrong. He exposed an important issue that many police officers were unwilling to acknowledge and posed questions that continue to resonate today. In essence, Rodney King, though badly brutalized as he lay near death on a Southeast Los Angeles street, made his ascent to expose to the world not only the reality of police racism and brutality, but the reality of police relations with African-American citizens, including those of American-metropolitan ghetto regions, where poverty is rampant.

It is instructive to note that Sir Robert Peel, founder of the London Metropolitan Police Department and from which American policing evolved, envisioned the ideal police officer as highly trained, calm, stable, quiet, determined, capable of controlling emotions and appearance, and able to generate the respect and bring honor to the police force. Contrary to the current situation where much of the success of law enforcement is assessed based on arrest rates, he strongly emphasized that police efficacy should be demonstrated by crime reduction through use of adequate crime prevention strategies, including police officer demeanor and temperament.

Law enforcement represents, as Thibault, Lynch, & McBride (2004) suggested, "big business." For example, during the year 2000, city, county, and state police agencies collectively employed 654,601 police officers to provide law enforcement services to 265 million people in the U.S. Most law enforcement officers are at the local level. In fact, the U.S. Department of Justice reported that 56% of the officers are assigned to police inner-city, lower-class regions — those areas with extremely high poverty rates. Regardless of assigned work location, one cannot overemphasize the significance of law enforcement for societal preservation. Equally important is the necessity for "improved relationship building" between the police and African-American minorities of the inner cities, especially those of the lower classes.

THE ROLE, MISSION AND DUTIES OF THE POLICE

Today, urban American (inner-city) communities, especially those heavily inhabited by lower-class minorities (blacks and hispanics), are more heavily patrolled and scrutinized by the police. Moreover, such locations reflect higher arrest, conviction, incarceration and recidivism rates (Bureau Justice Statistics, 1997). Of great importance is the necessity to understand the role and mission of law enforcement and its importance for the security, maintenance, and preservation of societal laws.

The basic purposes for policing American communities are to (1) enforce, support and uphold the laws of society; (2) investigate criminal activity and apprehend law violators; (3) prevent and control crime; (4) maintain and preserve the peace; and (5) provide various services to citizens. In studying police behavioral style, Wilson (1968) noted three (3) major policing styles, which were depictions representative of how a particular law enforcement agency comprehended its purpose and adopted various tactics to fulfill the mission. Wilson's three policing styles include (1) Watchman / order maintenance, where the police maintain order through informal intervention-type strategies consisting of persuasion, threats, or even employment of some aggressive behaviors; (2) Legalistic, where the police enforce the letter of the law; and (3) Service, where the police see themselves more as helpers than being embroiled in tumultuous encounters or in combat with citizens. While crime control is a legitimate role of state government, Omi and Winant (1986) cautions one to be cognizant about images and messages stemming from phrases such as "law and order" and "getting tough on crime," in that these can become a mechanism to conjure up images of dangerous people of color: In essence, they are code words — words that indirectly reference and stereotype African-American minorities.

Beckett and Sasson (2000) further cautioned about one's perception of the term "punitiveness," since it holds negative connotations of hostility toward African Americans who are disproportionately poor and socially isolated in poor communities where they are more susceptible to the criminal justice system. Generally speaking, they live where the police are more likely to patrol; thus the likelihood of being arrested, convicted, and incarcerated is greater.

POLICE OFFICER SUBCULTURE AND WORKING PERSONALITY

According to Tylor (1871), with whom many anthropologists have concurred, "Culture… is that complete whole which includes knowledge, belief, art, morals, law, custom, and any other capabilities and habits acquired by man as a member of society." The police, though part of the American culture as a whole, after completing academy-level training and donning the uniform with the badge, weapon, and baton stick, form their own clear and distinctive subculture. A subculture, as reported by Robertson (1987), is "a group that shares in the overall culture of society but also has its own distinctive values, norms, and lifestyle."

Within the police culture, there exists a clear and definitive set of cultural norms which Robertson defines as "shared rules or guidelines that proscribe the behavior appropriate in a given situation" (1987:62). These norms form the basis of a lifestyle for police officers, both on and off the job. When Westley (1970) studied the police of Gary, Indiana results revealed a police subculture characteristic of "secrecy" and "violence"; in fact, police officers viewed the public as their enemy. Additional findings depicted negative attitudes of the police toward citizens who disliked police, and reported that citizen hostility and disrespect for police led to increased violence against citizens, as well as greater police solidarity, secrecy, and lying.

The police officer's "working personality" is what Skolnick (1966) coined when observing police subcultural behavior, and noted that the elements of danger, authority, and efficiency were deeply rooted in the working world of the police officer. Specifically danger, he conceded, strongly influences the police officers' personality in that it is impossible to predict occurrences; consequently, they are trained to be circumspect, guarded, and alert when interacting with citizens. Not being cognizant of the backgrounds or the behavior patterns of citizens that police officers have to confront is apt to create suspicion; ultimately, this personality characteristic becomes deeply embedded in the personal lives of police officers. With police officer's duties comes "authority," which entails the power of the police to use persuasion, legal coercion, and legalized force. Also, the symbols alone — uniform, badge, weapon, and police vehicle — convey "police authority." With "efficiency," there is the demand from public officials and citizens to know that the police are working effectively and efficiently, with documented proof (paperwork) to demonstrate that the police are engaged in controlling and preventing crime and that nothing will hamper "real policing." Purpura (2001), however, cautioned that when police agencies become so preoccupied with proving their efficiency through paperwork and a culture of covering one's tracks, officers can lose sight of the actual goals of the organization. Hence, the police "working personality" reflects their steeped frustrations over an organization bowed to prove efficiency at the expense of public safety and crime prevention and control.

Additional characteristics of "the police working personality" have been reported by other researchers. Niederhoffer (1967), a former New York City Police Officer, for example, wrote in a report that police officers are cynical about both the community in which they police and the police department itself which employs them. Cynicism (a distrust of human nature and motives) begets authoritarianism, stereotyping, aggression, and a "we versus them" attitude, he concluded. Similarly, Purpura (2001) reported that the term "police subculture" alone when alluded to is suggestive of police not only being cynical and authoritarian, but also acting suspicious, prejudiced, hostile, secretive, honorable, loyal, efficient, and conservative. Such values and personality characteristics do influence how officers view their world and how they act.

Reporting on the police officer "code of secrecy," also known as the "blue curtain," Goldstein (1977) stated that this secrecy code is tighter in law enforcement than in other fields of employment. He furthermore remarked on factors that contribute to police subculture. These include:

- police see themselves as a group aligned against common enemies: when one is attacked, the entire group has fallen under attack;

- police place heavy dependency on each other in difficult and troublesome moments: thus, they cannot afford to report on the behaviors of their fellow officers;
- when faced with false allegations, police need and depend on the support from fellow officers;
- police are aware that formal policy versus actual practices that serve the public's interest will not stand the scrutiny test; consequently, any inappropriate behaviors by the police become masked; and
- with no occupational mobility, officers must anticipate working with the same individuals.

Subcultures entail groups of people within larger societies with their ways of living, norms, beliefs, attitudes, and values. The fact that a police subculture exists would suggest that the police are different from civilians and that such differences can be attributed to the working environment. Cole and Smith (2000) listed three prime ingredients pertinent to police subculture: police officer personality, social isolation, and stress. Specifically stated, police officer working personality becomes altered over time as officers increasingly are exposed to the threat of danger and forced to exert their authority over citizens who do not automatically acquiesce to their authority. Social isolation can result because of the nature of police work: officers are expected to live exemplary lives and should always be on duty; they separate themselves from civilians, personally and professionally; they use technical jargon when discussing work; and they utilize a "code system" when discussing police work details. Stress for officers can result from various stressors: organizational, police work itself, and personal. Hence, these can engender high rates of suicide, divorce, heart disease, alcohol and drug abuse.

All is not negative about police subculture: Crank (1997) commented on the value of police subculture, especially for community policing philosophy, where significant positive changes in police work can and must occur. Furthermore, he concluded that police subculture "is not something to be fixed" and that the police subculture is comprised of officers who do possess knowledge, skills, common sense, tradition, practical knowledge about trouble / hot spots, and a greater understanding of neighborhoods, including those of the inner cities. He maintains that these characteristics cannot be removed from police subculture, and even went further to assert the importance of experienced officers: he insisted that when planning for police reform, these officers must be included, not excluded (Crank, 1997).

POLICE USE OF DISCRETION

Fundamental to the role / authority of police work is the exercise of discretion. According to Purpura (2001), "discretion" is the ability to choose among various options before selecting a path of action, e.g., whether to use force; to use pepper spray; to refer a citizen to a "helping" agency; or to warn, scold, release, or make an arrest. Moreover, police discretion pivots on many factors such as current organization priorities, available evidence, and the seriousness of the situation.

While reflecting on police use of discretion, Robinson (2005) reported that police discretion is the ability of an officer to act according to his or her own sound professional judgment rather than on some established rules or procedures. It is an important dimension that provides the flexibility to improve job performance and public safety. The fact that archaic laws exist on the books that are not expected to be enforced as well as the lack of resources including officers to enforce all laws, most definitely illustrate the importance of police discretionary authority. Meanwhile, Jones-Brown and Terry (2004) deemed it a necessity to make the distinction between the use of "mere capacity" and "having / using" discretion for police decision making. Police are faced with many opportunities to exercise this judgment (make decisions) when responding to situations. However, the "mere capacity" to exercise judgment differs from that of "using discretion." Discretion is a prerogative (role entitlement), not just "mere capacity." Furthermore, it is a normative resource with authority; it is a type of social recognition bounded by legal constraints (laws), regulations, and standards. It does not encompass officers choosing whatever they want to do with impunity (Kleinig, 1996a). In spite of this, the discretionary power of the police is limited within the framework of the law (substantive, procedural), departmental regulations, and organizational supervisory guidelines. While discretion is an inevitable and a vital part of police work that offers considerable flexibility to officers in a variety of situations, there is a major concern about uncontrolled and unsupervised discretion, in that this could lead to police abuse of power, e.g., citizen abuse by police and other forms of police corruption. In a 1966 report issued by the National Association of Criminal Defense Lawyers, unchecked and unmonitored discretion usage by police engenders racial stereotypes that result in racial profiling and disparities, police use of force and other forms of citizen abuse and police corruption. Cox and Wade (1998) are of the opinion that granting police the awesome power of discretion is asking for trouble, especially when police are dishonest, partial, bigoted, and unethical. They further claimed:

> It is the existence of discretion by individual police officers in thousands of police-citizen encounters everyday that helps shape public attitudes toward the police ... If an officer arrests one person for a particular offense but allows another who has committed the same offense to go free, the arrested party ... can hardly be expected to feel that the criminal justice system is just. (Cox & Wade, 1998, p. 101)

Nonetheless, power is essential to the success of American policing: the concern is determining how to ensure that it will not be misused. Robinson (2005) strongly believes that when there is a heavy focus on combating street crime, the real goal of law enforcement of serving citizens, to control and prevent crime while upholding Constitutional protections, is not achieved effectively and efficiently.

CITIZEN DISSATISFACTION WITH POLICE
A total lack of "harmony" shown in the lexicon of police interaction with minority communities is how some criminologists have characterized the interface of the police and inner-city African American minorities

(Barlow & Barlow, 2000; Dantzker & Jones-Brown, 2004; Shusta, Levine, Harris, & Wong 2002). These authors further contended this relationship to be anything but harmonious — a situation that stemmed from the old slave patrol days to the enforcement of the old "Jim Crow" laws to the days of police power segregation or the days when Black officers could police blacks only in the absence of a white officer. This relationship, in general, consisted of considerable hostility and violence. Wadman and Allison (2004) pointed out that as uncomfortable as it may have seemed, policing in the South was primarily about ongoing pursuits of slaves, and that patrolling slaves proved to be a significant step in the development of Southern police organizations and practices. Consequently, this style of policing paved the way for entrenched policing practices to be grounded in racial violence and an ingrained police culture heavily rooted in slavery.

Hancock and Sharp (1997) also remarked on similarities noted with current patterns of police officers' abuse of their authority to use physical force to those adopted and used during the "old historical vigilante justice days," especially the lynchings, abusive forms of interrogation procedures with suspects (the "third degree"), as well as the inept, biased, and oppressive handling of large civil unrest. The excessive force tactics employed by police today, harbor the antecedents of underlying fear and disdain of African-American minorities, including those of metropolitan ghetto areas. Use of police brutality today under color of law (one's law enforcement duties) is definitely a means for the amplification of some of America's worst impulses or expressions of racism, of which police have always been and remain active participants (Hancock & Sharp, 1997). Concerned about the interaction of the police with inner city African-American minorities, Peak and Glensor (1999) listed seven sources of tension that permeate the relationship of police and African-American minorities as follows:

- when calling for police assistance, African-American minorities report greater delays with "police response time" than whites;

- experiences with verbal abuse and racially offensive epithets directed toward them by police; Peak and Glensor (1999) suggests this form of disrespect to be an expression of "alienation" by police used as a control strategy to establish their "authority";
- considerable exposure to "stop and frisk" and interrogation questioning tactics by police;
- discriminatory patterns of arrest and traffic citations noted;
- excessive use of "physical" force used against lower class black males. Such force procedures were used against black males by both Caucasian and African-American police officers, causing racial minorities to perceive their own ethnicity as being unduly brutalized.
- excessive use of deadly force directed toward African-American minorities; and
- underenforcement of the law: failure to provide adequate law enforcement services to African-Americans.

Further, in a report issued by the National Advisory Commission on Civil Disorders (1973), police treatment of inner city African-American minorities was listed as a significant factor that fueled acts of violence and property destruction across America. Today, little over thirty years later, African-American inner city minorities continue to have lower views of the police than any other group (Tuck & Weitzer, 1997).

While Peak and Glensor (2004) listed racism to be the leading cause of poor relations between the police and inner city African-American minorities, the highly renowned, National Academy of Sciences concluded more than a decade ago that the matter of blacks and criminality is related to past and present social inequities, which best can be understood through consideration of blacks' overall social status. Peak and Glensor (2004) went further to remark that with recent mass gatherings in Washington D.C., engineered by protest groups such as the Southern Christian Leadership Conference and the Rainbow Coalition to protest against racial profiling, police brutality and other perceived prejudices directed toward African-American minorities, such assemblies indicate that the Academy's statement and position is still valid today. As for many African-American minorities, they view the police as only an "occupying force," whose primary intention and concern is to restrict their freedom, not to provide services to their communities.

Unquestionably, some inner city African-American citizens take the position that the police have no redeeming qualities; they perceive the police officer to be symbolic of an unjust criminal justice system and should never be trusted. Of course, the most difficult of all policing problems entails making it clear and obvious as to what the basic regulatory nature of policing encompasses. Baldwin (1961) provides a classic and powerful description on how the police are viewed in America's ghetto regions:

> The only way to police a ghetto is to be oppressive. None of the Police Commissioner's men, even with the best will in the world, have any way of understanding the lives led by the people they swagger about in twos and threes controlling. Their very presence is an insult, and it would be, even if they spent their entire day feeding gumdrops to children. They represent the force of the White World, and that world's criminal profit and ease, to keep the black man corralled up here, in his place. The badge, the gun in the holster, and the swinging club make vivid what will happen should his rebellion become overt. He moves through Harlem, therefore, like an occupying soldier in a bitterly hostile country, which is precisely what and where he is, and is the reason he walks in twos and threes. (Baldwin, 1961, pp. 65–67).

Walker, Spohn, & Delone (2000), in addressing the concerns about police interaction with African-American inner-city minorities, noted that African-American minorities hold less favorable attitudes and opinions of the police than do Caucasians. They further remarked about the consistency of race and ethnicity as being the strongest determinant factors when forming attitudes about the police, and that the conflict existing between the police and African-American minorities is not a new phenomenon. These views were confirmed by other researchers: (Bureau of Justice Statistics, 1997; Lotz, 2005; Walker, 1997; Robinson, 2002; Tuck & Weitzer, 1997; Weisburg & Greenspan, 2002). Walker, et al. (2000) enumerated a myriad of reasons for African-American citizen discontentment with the police including police use of deadly force, police brutality, discriminatory practices with arrests, quality of life policing tactics, stopping, questioning, and frisking procedures, racial stereotyping including the "Driving While Black" phenomenon, verbal abuse including the use of racial or ethnic slurs, police prejudicial behavior, police corruption (drug trafficking, delinquency, gambling, prostitution), inadequate responses to citizen complaints, ineffectiveness of police community relations programs, lack of follow-up or investigation of citizen complaints against the police, and police employment practices.

JUVENILES' INTERACTION WITH THE POLICE

In assessing interaction between the police and juveniles, researchers have observed that African American minority youth, especially those who appear to be "tough guys" or to be affiliated with gangs are more likely than white youths to be stopped, interrogated, "roughed up," and arrested (Black & Reiss, 1970; Piliavin & Briar, 1964). Also, regardless of the seriousness of the criminality, juvenile inner city African-American minorities are more likely to be confronted by the police, arrested, detained, and referred to juvenile court (Dannefer & Schutt, 1982; Fagan, Slaughter, & Harlstone, 1987; Huzinga & Elliott, 1987).

While Simpson (1986) acknowledged race and social class as significant factors in determining police actions toward African-American minority youth, Ferdinand and Luchterhand (1970) did not find racism to be the leading cause of white police officers' indifferent attitudes toward African-American minority youth, but rather due to the lack of empathy and understanding for minority values and norms stemming from such disparate social and cultural backgrounds. Police are the most obvious and visible symbol representing the criminal justice system, standing out in the front lines. Juveniles having any involvement with criminal justice or juvenile justice officials will be initially confronted by the police, not the judges, probation or parole agents, prison, or other correctional institutions. Their contacts with the police may leave them with long-lasting impressions thus tarnishing their attitudes toward the police.

Of paramount importance is the question: How do juveniles rate the police? Normally, studies on juveniles' attitudes toward the police center on samples of high school students (Lotz, 2005). However, Leiber, Nalla, & Farnworth (1998) saw it more beneficial to assess attitudes of delinquents in training schools, detention centers, group homes, and treatment centers in that they had considerably more contact with the police than most youths. Nevertheless, youths with the least respect for the police were found to be those with delinquent attitudes; those who had to have considerable involvement with the Juvenile Justice System; those from high crime neighborhoods; and those most often taken to the station house (McCord, Widom, & Crowell, 2001).

In investigating juveniles' attitudes toward the police using high school students, Hurst (1993) found that juveniles had negative attitudes toward the police, that juveniles expressed distrust of the police, and strongly believed that the police were not effective at preventing crime. Negative attitudes about the police were found to be more pronounced among African-American than among white students.

TACTICAL COMMUNICATION

Just as citizens express concerns about police officers' negative behaviors toward them, so have the police advanced their concerns about citizens' use of inappropriate behaviors directed toward them. While major goals of police work include soliciting information from citizens without being confrontational and eliciting voluntary compliance from citizens without use of physical force, Meese and Ortmeier (2004) highly recommended police officers' use of "tactical communication," in that it is a message conveyed through words and actions for accomplishing these goals. Additionally, police officers' demeanor should always be professional, respectful and unbiased recognizing that any encounter is potentially dangerous.

Meese and Ortmeier (2004) cautioned police officers to remain calm in their encounters with angry, hostile, hysterical, or emotionally unstable citizens and recognize that speaking in a harsh or negative tone may cause the matter to intensify. They specifically suggested that very young individuals, upon officer confrontation, could become easily frightened and confused while more elderly individuals might miscomprehend instructions. Meese and Ortmeier (2004) further strengthened their recommendation for voluntary compliance through "tactical communication" to be achieved through adherence of the following:

- give the citizen the opportunity to comply voluntarily;
- explain the problem within the context of the law and provide reason(s) for requesting voluntary compliance;
- explain options to citizens, outlining possible courses of action and consequences of each;
- request cooperation and provide citizens with one final opportunity for compliance; and
- if citizens fail to comply with police officer's request(s), then appropriate action must be taken—action that is congruent with the law and police agency policy.

Police officers are often subjected to verbal and physical abuse by citizens. Shusta, et al. (2005) reported that many officers feel that their lives are in danger when policing metropolitan inner city ghetto regions where poverty and crime go hand in hand, where police feel that they are expected to solve major societal ills, including heavy crime fighting, without adequate training to deal with such problems that are deeply rooted in historical, social, political and economic factors. The following was stated:

Many policemen find themselves on the alert for the slightest sign of disrespect... Likewise, the attitudes and emotions of the black citizen may be similar when confronted with a police [officer]. Intervention by police is often seen as an infringement on the black's rights

and as oppression by the white population. Consequently
many blacks are on the alert for the slightest sign of
disrespect that might be displayed by the police [officer].
(Shusta et al., 2005, pp. 179–180).

Cross and Renner (1974) explained that it's both the fear of
belittlement and danger that cause not only the police but African-
American inner city citizens as well to misinterpret what might otherwise
be non-threatening behavior. "Mutual fear" is what generates this type
of behavior and although Cross and Renner's ideas were crafted in the
early 1970s, their findings still hold true today (Shusta, et al. 2005).
Interestingly, Black (1971), found that race was not a factor for arrest
decisions, but rather, a matter that evolved from African-American
minorities' display of disrespect toward the police, thus confirming the
findings of Cox and Wade (1998) that African-American minorities are
uncooperative with the police and openly hostile many times.

From another point of view, when Son, Davis, and Rome (1998)
investigated the extent to which a suspect's race influenced police behavior,
results confirmed those of Black (1971) that suspects' disrespect of police
officers, not race, influenced the officer's decision to effectuate an arrest.
Meanwhile, African-American police officers experience an added problem:
Inner-city African-American minorities label them as "traitors" of their
own African American race because they became police officers
(McNamara, 2004). Hunter, Barker, & Mayhall (2004) suggest that the
police will continue to be viewed by many inner city African-American
minorities as representatives of a system that is unjust, unfair, and
oppressive. McNamara (2004), on the other hand, supports the notion
that in some locations race is a major factor in determining who is more
apt to be the subject of verbal abuse, stop-and-frisk police behaviors and
other inappropriate police action. However, he contends that police
discretion and subculture are the basis for the negative treatment of inner
city African-American minorities by the police.

COMMUNICATION AND MULTICULTURAL RELATIONSHIPS

Approximately 70 percent of a police officer's work day involves communicating with citizens, superiors, fellow officers, governmental officials, and others. According to Wallace, Robertson and Steckler (2001) and Whisenand and Ferguson (2002), "proficiency" for police-officer communication, verbal or nonverbal, is greatly needed. In investigating the effectiveness of "good communicators," Anderson (2000) revealed that fewer than one in three individuals claiming to be good communicators could actually demonstrate their ability to use effective communication skills during a live competence assessment procedure. Anderson (2000) further noted that those assessed were shown to be very deficient in difficult-to-learn counseling, coaching, and consultative skills. In another study of police communication effectiveness, Ortmeier (1996) strongly confirmed "effective communication skills" as being crucial to the success of law enforcement.

While numerous definitions of communication exist, communication in its basic form is more of a process than an event in which at least two individuals are engaged in information exchange. This process consists of transmitting, receiving, and sharing ideas, facts, attitudes, values, and opinions (Meese & Ortmeier, 2004).

Communication is fast becoming a significant focus of law enforcement. For example, interpersonal communication (person-to-person interaction) occurs when a police officer is confronted with a disturbance like domestic violence. He can either defuse the matter or cause it to escalate to a more serious situation. Escalation may provoke brutality and place the police officer himself at risk or cause an unnecessary arrest. Person-to-group communication as suggested by Hunter, et al. (2004) implies a more structured situation where one person addresses a group about a predetermined subject. An example might be the law enforcement officer serving as a witness before a jury or addressing school violence prevention before a local school board.

With official communication, the focus is most often written but can give the appearance of person-to-person or group-to-person interaction. This type of communication is usually "public" documentation of policy or procedure, or evaluative reports, and so on. Equally important, this includes police officers' communication about their response to reported crime incidences through complaint or incident format procedures. Commenting more on police officer interpersonal communication, Hunter, et al. (2004) advised a three-channel mode framework for interpersonal skills interaction. First is verbal, which almost always encompasses words and combinations of words for message transmittal or even for feedback. In essence, words in and of themselves are meaningless. However, meaning can be derived from the individual or from within the context from which words are used. Second, the nonverbal mode is comprised of three important subgroups: (1) paralanguage or vocal characteristics that consist of a police officer's diction, rate and pitch and / or speech loudness or softness; (2) kinesics (police officer body language) that includes gestures, body positioning, facial expressions, movement, and so on; (3) proxemics that centers on how the police use personal space — space which could be a territorial issue (neighborhood problem) or a privacy intrusion concern; and (4) symbolic communication or communication considered more of a nonverbal entity rather than a separate communication channel; the communication is continuous and passive. More often than not, symbolic communication includes messages about one's style of dress, place of residence, place and type of employment, type of car driven or mode of preferred transportation, type of jewelry worn, beard worn, and others. Moreover, law enforcement makes use of numerous symbols: uniform, nightstick, the revolver, badge. The uniform itself is symbolic of authority and in situations where officers are respected and in command, the uniform alone will attest positively to police-citizen interaction. On the contrary, if police are regarded as enemies or as scapegoats, the uniform then becomes a negative symbolic cue, thus thwarting any positive police-citizen interaction.

IMPEDIMENTS TO EFFECTIVE POLICE–CITIZEN COMMUNICATION

Importantly, blocks to effective police communication have been documented. Wallace, et al. (2001) suggest the presence of emotional and physical barriers, ineffective listening, and lack of a common meaning concerning a word or phrase (semantic problems). Other factors that impede effective police communication are featured by Hunter, et al. (2004) and include: (1) community distrust of police; police distrust of citizens; (3) inadequate training of police; (4) the organizational structure of the police agency; and (5) scapegoating (simple preferences, active biases, prejudice, discrimination, and full-fledged scapegoating are steps that illustrate the process of "scapegoating.")

Community Distrust of Police
When citizens place little trust in the police, they will be less apt to interact with the police. Therefore, they will be less cooperative in helping the police solve crimes.

Police Distrust of Community
When police perceive the community as dangerous, they may refrain from protecting community members. This will exacerbate tensions and widen the gap between the police and citizens of the community.

Inadequate Police Officer Training
While police officer training has improved significantly in recent years, academy level police officer training is still heavily built around those skills essential to perform only the basics of law enforcement. A study by Strawbridge and Strawbridge (1990) found that only two of the 80 police departments surveyed devoted approximately 20 percent of academy level training to interpersonal skills development. The majority of training time was spent on basic police procedures: law, weapons training, driver training, self-defense, and first aid.

Conflict management and sensitivity skills training were two components of interpersonal skills training that were the least taught in all academies, even in those which offered more hours toward interpersonal skills training. Consequently, dedicated and responsible police officers are assigned to street level patrol duty without adequate preparation for the experiences they will encounter. They lack a clear understanding of citizens' attitudes, an appreciation of historical and cultural factors that shape the larger community, and the necessary training to defuse dangerous situations. Additionally, they lack the training needed to adequately respond to threats, hostility, or force involving their duties. Also, lack of police officer training of specific subjects were shown to impede effective police officer communication. These include the following: Introduction to Social Theory, Basic Psychology, Human Development and Behavior, Minority History, Constitutional Law, Ethnic Studies, Interpersonal Relations, and Communication Skills.

Organizational Structure

According to Hunter, et al. (2004), the majority of U.S. police departments are organized paramilitary style, with command chains, defined areas of responsibility, volumes of rules and regulations, and also a clear membership hierarchy and ranking systems. Bittner (1970) views this style of organizational structure to be paradoxical in nature in that it strengthens command authority but does very little for the operations of police departments since police managers and supervisors do not direct police office activities in any important sense; they are perceived as mere disciplinarians.

Scapegoating

Allport (1954) sees scapegoating as a concept wherein some aggressive behaviors of an individual or group are directed toward a particular individual, group, or object, with the use and amount of aggression and blame not being fully substantiated. More specifically, police target particular individuals or groups even though such attention is unwarranted.

Simple Preferences

Hunter, et al. (2004) remarked that "simple preferences" can impact interactions. People have preferences and tend to favor individuals who agree with them or share similar backgrounds and values.

Active Biases

In this case, the simple preferences become altered and much stronger. An individual or group's "simple preference" proceeds to a negative state. The active bias state then moves closer toward a closed mind and full-blown prejudice.

Prejudice:

According to Hunter, et al. (2004), being prejudiced or having prejudices, prejudging certain groups, individuals or events is not an uncommon phenomenon. Prejudice, they warned, is not a major threat to society as long as it is not acted upon. Also, when people are involved in public safety, such as law enforcement, it becomes extremely difficult not to allow prejudice to impact one's judgment.

Discrimination:

Discrimination as suggested by Hunter, et al. (2004) is an act of exclusion stemming from prejudice. Employment, housing, health care, and other social institutions are areas where discrimination is often manifested. Some police officers still perceive minorities, including the African-American, as unworthy, unwanted, and unacceptable human beings.

Full-Fledged Scapegoating:

Scapegoating, as shown by Hunter, et al. (2004) manifests itself after all prior steps have taken place. It involves concentrated aggression against individuals or groups. Hunter, et al. (2004) cautioned police departments to carefully screen its applicants to identify individuals who may be inclined toward scapegoating behaviors. Applicants fitting this category are apt to become serious liabilities to law enforcement. Therefore, attempts must be made to ensure that such applicants do not slip through the screening process. There is the danger that such an officer might use excessive force. When such force is unwarranted, communication breakdown between the police and the community can occur.

Skills that focus on "Emotional Intelligence" associated with the "Affective Domain" or more specifically "feelings" of empathy or empathic concern for individuals are essential to police work. The idea is not to turn police officers into social workers, as crime fighting and prevention are necessary requirements in a society. However, support of improved communication skills for the nation's law enforcement officers focusing on empathy, would help them become more people-oriented and caring.

THE POLICE AND THE AFRICAN-AMERICAN (BLACK) CULTURE

In addition to understanding their own police subculture, the police need to appreciate the nature and importance of the African-American culture. From a communication standpoint, culture refers to a group's beliefs, language, actions, and artifacts (Kidd & Braziel, 1999; Putnam & Pacanowski, 1983). It is not what a group has, but rather what a group is. Swanson, Territo and Taylor (2005) advised that while culture is applicable to various population categories, race and ethnicity comprise the mix most often associated with culture.

Though the problems associated with the racial aspects of black-white relations in American society have been and continue to be overwhelming and to a great extent eclipse cultural differences between white and black Americans, the effects of slavery and discrimination should not be deemphasized. The African-American culture is strongly influenced by African culture and it is significantly different from the Caucasian culture.

Many police superiors realize that with an influx of immigrants, officers are better equipped to establish trust, communicate effectively and experience mutual cooperation so long as they have basic knowledge and understanding of the group's cultural background. Unfortunately, past history reveals that cultural differences are seldom considered, even with the understanding that culturally related misperceptions can and do cause serious communication problems between these citizens and the police.

African Americans, though no longer the largest minority within the United States still comprise 12.3 percent of the U. S. population and reside primarily within the nation's urbanized regions. Moreover, they constitute approximately 22.1 percent of all persons living below the poverty level (U.S. Bureau of Census, 2000). Hunter, et al. (2005) caution that such figures may be interpreted to mean that African Americans are overly represented within the lower classes in the inner cities. As a consequence, large numbers of African-Americans experience severe economic and social hardships that place a direct burden on relations between themselves and the police.

Despite the considerable progress made with regard to race relations in American society, African-Americans continue to be disproportionately represented within the criminal justice system with high arrest, conviction, and incarceration rates. Researchers contend that although African-Americans have for the most part become culturally assimilated into the American culture as a whole, adopting American behaviors, customs, language, dress, and values, many resist becoming integrated and accepted into the common institutional and social life of American society (Vander Zanden, 1983; Marger, 1996). This resistance to structural assimilation can be linked to "lingering ethnocentrism" among both the white majority and African-Americans.

Much of the difficulty faced by African-Americans in becoming assimilated into the U.S. society entails notable racial characteristics and the legacy of slavery (Hunter, et al., 2004). Yet, the African-American culture is extremely rich and varied in all of its manifestations. Failing to acknowledge the distinctiveness of the African-American culture can lead to misunderstanding, conflict, and confrontations. There is a need for the police to be cognizant of the history of African-American minorities as they interact with the citizens of America's inner city regions.

RELATIONSHIP-BUILDING SUGGESTIONS FOR POLICE AND INNER-CITY, AFRICAN-AMERICAN MINORITIES

Accompanying the American system of democracy are several defining features that include the provision of equal protection of all citizens from unjust, repressive, and arbitrary tactics of state abuse and violence, as well as the need for those charged with enforcement of the law to do so with the highest degree of honor and respect. However, when breaches do occur, those representing "authority" must adopt and adhere to measures that ensure both symbolic and material redress. It is of paramount importance that steps be effectuated to improve interaction with African-American inner-city minorities and, simultaneously, to assist the citizens in developing more trust, respect, and allegiance to the police. Towards this, the following issues should be addressed:

- organization change;
- police administration, organization, and leadership;
- police officer recruitment, screening, and selection;
- police officer training: pre-service and in-service; and
- improve relations with African-American minorities.

ORGANIZATIONAL CHANGE

Organizational change occurs when police departments adopt and implement new ideas, strategies, or behaviors. Change within the police organization involves the attempt to persuade police officers to alter their behavior and relationships with one another or others. While a small percentage of police officers are apt to embrace change, the majority, approximately 80%, will wait until fully convinced or until the change itself is unavoidable. This was witnessed when attempting to implement a first-time prison volunteer program in a maximum security prison, while serving in a supervisory capacity. Once correctional officers saw that the program was working, then it was extolled. Because of the correctional agency's strong endorsement of the change, others followed as directed. According to Lewin (1958) the three-phase process for planned change — "Unfreezing," "Changing," and "Refreezing" — can be of great benefit to police managers when attempting to establish change. With "Unfreezing" the police department can overcome negative obstacles that create resistance to change due to new or daunting information. "Changing" is about changing attitudes, values, feelings, and behaviors of the police or citizens when new actions are planned and discussed. "Refreezing" occurs when the police organization arrives at a

new status quo with support procedures intact to maintain the desired
behaviors or changes.

ADMINISTRATION, LEADERSHIP, AND IMPROVING RELATIONSHIPS

It is essential to conceptualize the organizational structure of U.S.
police departments including those of urban areas. They are paramilitary
structured with command chains, defined areas of responsibility, volumes
of rules and regulations, and a clear hierarchy of membership. In police
organizations, there are chiefs, deputy chiefs, captains, sergeants, and
patrol officers. Many large police organizations carry the ranks further
to include colonel, major, and corporal. Bittner (1970) described this
form of paramilitary structure for police organizations as follows:

> Another complex of mischievous consequences arising
> out of the military bureaucracy relates to the paradoxical
> fact that while this kind of discipline ordinarily
> strengthens command authority it has the opposite effect
> in police departments. This effect is insidious rather
> than apparent. Because police superiors do not direct
> the activity of officers in any important sense, they are
> perceived as mere disciplinarians (Bittner, 1970, p.
> 59).

Bittner (1970), in this instance, sees the army officer with the duty
to lead others into battle, even though the opportunity may not present
itself. Thus, the behavior of ranked police officials is perceived as
analogous to the army officer: someone who can only do a great deal
to subordinates, but very little for them. Bittner (1970) further contends
that this can create more harm than good for the police organization in
that it causes patrol officers to view their supervisors with distrust and
contempt. Also, effective communication becomes hampered within the
organization because of the superior/subordinate relationship—a relationship that becomes transferred to contacts or interaction between patrol

officers and, in this case, African-American, inner-city residents. A solution to the paramilitary model is to implement use of the community policing model whereby the community would set the police agenda. Police middle managers and line officers would become empowered through a close working relationship with community groups relevant to the community's agenda. The following are additional strategies for improving police organizations to enhance police and inner city African-American relationships:

- develop a reward system that places high value on an individual's accomplishments and excellent communication efforts;
- provide opportunities for exchange to occur between police officers and top level administrators;
- require mandatory training seminars for all key management and personnel line officers about community partnering for improved relationship building between the police and African-American, inner-city minorities; and
- incorporate use of the quality-circle concept into the organization to ensure the value of all, including top management and line police officers (Culliver, 1989).

POLICE OFFICER RECRUITMENT, SCREENING, AND SELECTION

The careful screening of police officer applicants is critical to alleviate and eliminate improper police behavior. In other words, weeding out those who are unfit for law enforcement work through effective screening and selection procedures can prevent police departments from problems such as excessive force and discriminatory behavior directed toward citizens. Importantly, individuals desiring to become police officers need to possess a very special communication quality — empathy. Different from the development of voice or listening skills, empathy is aesthetic. This quality is greatly needed by those entering police-oriented professions. It is a caring attitude, along with the capacity to comprehend the feelings, attitudes, and sentiments of others. It is what can be termed "compassionate policing"; it is an excellent strategy for defusing volatile situations.

Levin and Fox (1985) cautioned those screening police applicants to be vigilant in detecting those who lack the ability to comprehend another's feelings, attitudes, and sentiments. In extreme cases such individuals are "sociopathic" or "psychopathic" personalities in that they are incapable of experiencing love or empathy. Individuals can become sociopathic or psychopathic because of family rejection. Since the ability to form adequate bonds is impaired, sociopaths are apt to cheat, lie, or steal, or even commit criminal acts such as rape, murder, or aggravated assault. Also of importance is the need for those screening and selecting police applicants to be cognizant of applicants who have experienced deep insecurities, who have been unsuccessful with employment, who have developed an inferiority complex, or who have self-esteem problems. Additional recommended strategies are to place more emphasis on the applicant's "character" and screen for those with deep-seated racism or multi-cultural problems. In addition, the extension of police officer probationary periods for a longer time period, for example, up to three years, should be considered.

POLICE OFFICER TRAINING: ACADEMY LEVEL PRE-SERVICE AND IN-SERVICE

Widespread use of the police academy to train police recruits for new responsibilities continues to be a common feature of police departments throughout America. In addition, the state mandated required training for the police rookie is primarily provided through regional police academies, and more recently, post secondary institutions, particularly community colleges. Following a "boot camp" training model, the curriculum content agenda has been more oriented toward physical prowess, administration of justice, basic law, police procedures, and police proficiency. Recent training additions, although on a very limited basis, now encompass communication skills development, sensitivity, cultural, and ethnic-diversity training, and conflict resolution management. Also, once leaving the academy, training is extended to include "field level training."

Despite the training provided police rookies, Thibault, et al. (2004) reported that police officers' negative relations with inner city African-American minorities, citizen groups, and other ethnic groups reflect a major need for improved training. Consequently, the following recommendations are provided:

1. Replace the boot camp militaristic style training model with one that centers on adult learning techniques — those which focus on "adult learning principles" proposed by Knowles, (1990), which views adult learners to be autonomous and self-directed, with the ability to serve as active participants in the learning process;

2. Use the "problem-based learning (PBL)" curriculum that provides critical and analytical skills development. According to Peak and Glensor (2004), PBL is widely used in all aspects of police training including at the academy level for FTO training, and for instructor development courses designed to teach police officers to train other officers;

3. Provide additional training to include a stronger focus on "social work in policing," or what can be viewed as "compassionate policing" or empathic concern and development necessary to defuse issues such as racism, stereotyping, and others;

4. Encourage more police officer training at the higher education level; officers should be encouraged to pursue at least the four-year degree program;

5. Provide training about community-oriented policing programs and strategies to improve interaction of police and inner city African-American citizens including juveniles; and

6. Update police recruits' knowledge and understanding of the "best practices" for controlling and preventing crime for youths and adults.

IN-SERVICE AND ONGOING TRAINING

Given the myriad of problems and concerns by citizens about police behaviors such as poor communication, cultural insensitivity, disrespect, use of force, biased attitudes, scapegoating, and so on, it is critical that police receive adequate and continuous in-service training.

Peak (2001) stated the necessity of police officer training noting that police managers can be held liable for failure to provide adequate training to officers. Training can be accomplished via numerous strategies such as roll-call to cover new information, policies and procedural updates, in-service courses of shorter or longer duration, and using computerized training modules.

RECOMMENDED TRAINING TO IMPROVE RELATIONS WITH AFRICAN-AMERICAN MINORITIES

Interpersonal Skills Development: A Suggested Training Focus

- Stress management and reduction, including use of biofeedback relaxation.
- Anger-control management, using a Cognitive-Behavioral approach.
- Ethnic and Cultural Diversity Training, including sensitizing against stereotyping.
- Empathic skills development.
- Effective listening strategies.
- Self-esteem /concept enhancement and positive self-enhancement.
- Interpersonal communication skills development.
- Role playing with interpersonal feedback to permeate training endeavors.

The following strategies are designed to achieve mutual respect for inner city minorities and the police:

Strategies Designed to Achieve Mutual Respect for Inner City Minorities and the Police

- Strengthen community policing focus to make use of shared decision making between citizens and police.
- Adopt ride-along programs that involve not only the youth and adults who already have respect for the police but also include those who are disrespectful and distrustful of police.
- Establish and support creative educational liaison projects, working through local schools and churches.
- Provide opportunities for more "volunteerism" in policing.
- Provide cultural awareness training — using methods such as simulation exercises, role playing, and group activities to modify police officers' and citizens' attitudes and behaviors.
- Provide training to enhance effective listening skills.
- Use training techniques to improve crisis and conflict management resolution.
- Include training to improve skills for interacting with negative and angry individuals. Provide training that specifically targets various types of angry individuals including techniques and strategies for dealing with them.
- Provide training to improve ethics for sound decison making.

It is imperative that police agencies adopt use of the most promising community-based strategies to improve the negative relationships between the police and inner city African-American minorities, a relationship that has permeated American policing over the years.

Sutherland and Cressey (1974) acknowledged that police have been severely criticized and that the public takes a dispassionate attitude toward police problems. Noting that high police morale accrues from positive relations with citizens, Sutherland and Cressey (1974) suggested use of the Police-Community Relations model. The model, produced and organized by police, was designed to create / produce understanding with the public including African-American minorities. Importantly, the President's Commission on Law Enforcement and Administration of Justice (1967:100), remarked on the following: 1) that both citizen hostility toward police and police indifference or maltreatment of citizens are disruptive to law and order in society; 2) that citizens of inner city ghetto areas will not be afforded the necessary police protection until police feel welcome and their problems are better understood; 3) that improved cooperation between citizen unrest and the police should be relegated to police officers — those sworn to protect the community; 4) that to preserve peace, full citizen participation in law enforcement is extremely important; 5) that negative feelings only create added tension and irrational responses for inner-city, African-American minorities and the police. The President's Commission further stated that a Police Community Relations program is an important function of any police department in communities with substantial minority populations. The Commission concluded by providing the following recommendations:

Suggested/Recommended Strategies to Improve Interaction between the Police and Inner City African American Minorities

- establish within police departments special "Police-Community Relations" units with a problem-solving focus that is proactive;
- provide officers of the special PCR units with specialized race relations and human relations training;
- provide structured meetings and training sessions with citizens about the role and function of the police, and the importance of citizen participation;
- incorporate use of programs designed to improve police and citizen relations such as the program titled "Courtesy, Professionalism, and Respect" (CPR, implemented in 1997 by the New York City Police Department);
- adopt use of Citizen Police Academies for both youth and adults;

- provide forum sessions for youths and adults, using guest speakers: clergy, local college and university officials, civic groups, and school officials;
- provide youth and adults with simulated-type experiences about police work;
- provide citizens with specific training sessions with regard to anger control, conflict resolution/management, and crime prevention strategies;
- provide citizens with "Police Ride-Along" opportunities; and
- sponsor "Friendly Officer Day" programs through neighborhood schools and churches.

CONCLUSIONS

A serious strained relationship exists between the police and African-American minorities of inner-city regions. While racism and discrimination were alluded to as causal factors to explain this tumultuous relationship between the police and inner city residents, it is believed that research is too inconclusive to allege racism as a prime factor. Moreover, America's inner city areas are heavily inhabited by poorer lower classes and the inequalities experienced by them could result from poverty. Thus, the issue may be more related to "classism" than to "racism."

Relationship-building strategies that have been suggested must be implemented to improve interaction. Equally important is the need for a holistic-type approach to be adopted (family, school, clergy, criminal justice including the juvenile justice system, higher education, and others) to alter the negative relationship that has existed over the years.

Training plans to eradicate stereotyping, scapegoating, and others associated with inner-city policing must be implemented and should be ongoing. It is imperative that training strategies target both the police and citizens, including the youth, so that police might be viewed more positively.

Effective communication skills for improved cross-cultural relations with African-American, inner-city minorities are crucial for law enforcement officers to improve relations with citizens representing the many cultures in the American society.

REFERENCES

Allport, G. W. (1954). *The nature of prejudice.* New York: Doubleday.

Anderson, T. D. (2000). *Every officer is a leader: Transforming leadership for police justice, and public safety.* New York: St. Lucie Press.

Beckett, K., & Sasson, T. (2000). *The politics of injustice: Crime and punishment in America.* Thousand Oaks, CA: Pine Ridge Press.

Baldwin, J. (1961). *Nobody knows my name.* New York: Dial Press.

Barlow, D. E., & Barlow, M.H. (2000). *Police in a Multicultural society — an American story.* Prospect Heights, Ill.: Waveland Press.

Bittner, E. (1970). *The functions of the police in modern society.* Bethesda, MD: National Institute of Mental Health.

Black, D. (1971). *The social organization of arrest.* Stanford Law Review 23, 1087–1111.

Black, D. J., & Reiss, A. J., Jr. (1970). *Police control of juveniles. American Sociological Review* 35, 63–77.

Blauner, R. (1972). *Racial oppression in America.* New York: Harper & Row.

Bureau of Justice Statistics. *Sourcebook of Criminal Justice Statistics,* (1997), p. 107.

Cole, G., & Smith, C. (2000). *The American system of criminal justice,* Belmont, CA: Wadsworth.

Cox, S., & Wade, J. (1998). *The criminal justice network: An introduction.* New York: McGraw-Hill.

Crank, J. (1997). Celebrating Agency Culture: Engaging traditional Cop's Heart in Organizational Change. In Quint Thurman and Edmund McGarrell (Eds.). *Community Policing in a rural setting.* Cincinnati, OH: Anderson.

Cross, S., & Renner, E. (1974). An interaction analyses of police-black relations. *Journal of Police Science Administration,* 2 (1).

Culliver, C. (December 1989). Increasing correctional officer motivation the quality circle way. *Journal of Correctional Training.*

Dannefer, D., & Schutt, R. (1982). Race and juvenile justice processing in court and police agencies. *American Journal of Sociology* 87, 1113–1132.

Dantzker, M.L., & Jones-Brown, D.D. (2004). Policing and minority communities: An introduction to the exploration. In D. Jones-Brown & K. Terry, (Eds.). *Policing and minority communities.* Upper Saddle River, NJ: Prentice Hall.

Fagan, J., Slaughter, E., & Hartstone, E. (1987). Blind justice? The impact of race on the juvenile justice process. *Crime and Delinquency* 33, 224–258.

Ferdinand, T. N., & Luchterhand, E.G. (1970). Inner city youth, the police, the juvenile court, and justice. *Social Problems* 17, 510–527.

Goldstein, H. (1977). *Policing a free society.* Cambridge, MA: Ballinger.

Hancock, B.W., & Sharp, P.M. (1997). *Public policy crime and criminal justice.* Upper Saddle River, NJ: Prentice Hall.

Hunter, R.D., Barker, T., & Mayhall, P.P. (2004). *Police-community relations and the administration of justice.* Upper Saddle River, N.J.: Prentice Hall.

Hurst, N. (1993). *Managing cultural diversity in law enforcement by the year 2003* (order 16–0818). Sacramento, CA: Post Commission.

Huzinga, D., & Elliott, D.S. (1987). Juvenile offenders: Prevalence, offender incidence, and arrest rates by race. *Crime and Delinquency* 33: 206–223.

Kidd, V., & Braziel, R. (1999). *Community oriented policing cop talk: Essential communication skills for community policing.* San Francisco: Acada Books.

Kleinig, J. (1996a). Handling discretion with discretion. In J. Kleinig, (Ed.), *Handled with discretion: Ethical issues in police decision making* (pp.1–12). New York: Rowman & Littlefield.

Knowles, M.S. (1990). *The adult learner: A neglected species.* Houston, TX: Gulf Publishing Company.

Leiber, M.S., Nalla, M.K., & Farnworth, W. (1998). Explaining juveniles' attitudes toward the police. *Justice Quarterly* 15 (1), 151–74.

Levin, J., & Fox, J.A. (1985). *Mass Murder: America's Growing Menace.* New York: Plenum Press.

Lewin, K. (1958), Group decision and social change. In E. Maccoby, T. Newcomb, & E. Hartley (Ed.), *Readings in Social Psychology.* New York: Holt, Rinehart and Winston.

Lotz, R. (2005). *Youth crime in America.* Upper Saddle River, New Jersey: Prentice Hall.

Marger, M.(1996). *Race and ethnic relations: American and global perspectives.* Belmont, Calif.: Wadsworth.

Meese, E., & Ortmeier, P. (2004). *Leadership, ethics, and policing.* Upper Saddle River, N.J.: Prentice Hall

McCord, J., Widom, C., & Crowell, D. (2001). *Juvenile Crime, Juvenile Justice: Panel on Juvenile Crime, Prevention, Treatment and control.* Washington, D.C.: National Academy Press.

McNamara, R.P. (2004). Revering some, reveling others. In D. Jones-Brown, & K. Terry (Eds.), *Policing and minority communities: Bridging the gap.* Upper Saddle River, NJ: Prentice Hall.

National Advisory Commission on Civil Disorders (1973).

National Association of Criminal Defense Lawyers. (1996). *Racism in the criminal justice system.* Washington, DC: National Association of Criminal Defense Lawyers.

Niederhoffer, A. (1967). *Behind the shield: The police in urban society.* Garden City, NY: Doubleday.

Omi, M., & Winant, H. (1986). *Racial formation in the united states.* New York: Routledge and Kegan Paul.

Ortmeier, P. (1996). *Community policing leadership: A study to identify essential competencies.* Ann Arbor MI: University Microfilms International (Bell & Howell Information and Learning) Dissertation Services.

Peak, K. (2001). *Justice administration, police, courts and corrections management.* Upper Saddle River, NJ: Prentice Hall.

Peak, K.J., & Glensor, R.W. (2004). *Community policing and problem solving.* Upper Saddle River, New Jersey: Prentice Hall.

Peak, K., & Glensor, R. (1999). *Community policing and problem solving.* Upper Saddle River, NJ: Prentice-Hall.

Piliavin, J., & Briar, S. (1964). "Police encounters with juveniles," *American Journal of Sociology* 70.

The President's Commission on Law Enforcement and Administration of Justice. (1967). *The Challenge of Crime in Free Society.* Washington, DC: United States Government Printing Office.

Purpura, P.P. (2001). *Police and community.* Allyn & Bacon MA: Needham Heights.

Putnam, L., & Pacanowski, M. (Eds.). (1983) *Communication and organizations: An interpretive approach.* Beverly Hills, CA: Sage Publications.

Robertson, I. (1987). *Sociology* (3rd ed.). New York: Worth.

Robinson, M. (2002). *Justice Blind? Ideals and Realities of American criminal justice.* Upper Saddle River, NJ: Prentice Hall.

Robinson, M.B. (2005). *Justice Blind.* Upper Saddle River, New Jersey: Prentice Hall.

Shelden, R. (2001). *Controlling the dangerous classes.* Boston: Allyn & Bacon.

Shusta, R., Levine, O., Harris, P.R., & Wong, H.Z. (2002). *Multicultural law enforcement: Strategies for peacekeeping in a diverse society.* Upper Saddle River, N.J.: Prentice Hall.

Shusta, R., Levine, D., Wong, H., & Harris, P. (2005). *Multicultural law enforcement.* Prentice Hall: New Jersey.

Simpson, A. E. (1977). *The literature of police corruption*, Volume 1. New York: John Jay Press.

Simpson, R. (1986). Effects of socioeconomic context on official reaction to juvenile delinquency. *American Sociological Review* 51 (December), 876–885

Skolnick, J. (1966). *Justice without trial: Law enforcement in a democratic society.* New York: John Wiley.

Son, I., Davis, M., & Rome, D. (1998). Race and its effect on police officers' perceptions of misconduct. *Journal of Criminal Justice* 26 (1): 21–28.

Strawbridge, P., & Strawbridge, D. (1990). *A networking guide to recruitment, selection and probationary training.* Department of the United States of America. New York: John Jay College.

Sutherland, D., & Cressey, D. (1974). *Criminology* 9th ed. Philadelphia: J.B. Lippincott.

Swanson, C.R., Territo, L., & Taylor, R.W. (2005). Police administration. Upper Saddle River, New Jersey: Prentice Hall.

Tabb, W. (1970). *The political economy of the black ghetto.* New York: W.W. Norton.

Thibault, E. (2004). Proactive police management. Upper Saddle River, N.J.: Prentice Hall.

Thibault, E. A., Lynch, L.M., & McBride, R.B. (2004). *Proactive police management.* Upper Saddle River, N.J.: Prentice Hall.

Tuck, S., & Weitzer, R. (1997). Racial differences in attitudes toward the police, *Public Opinion Quarterly* 61, 643–663.

Tylor, E.B. (1871). *Primitive Culture.* London: John Murray.

U.S. Department of Justice. (1999). Use of force by police: Overview of National and Local Data. Washington, DC: United States Government Printing Office.

Vander Zanden, J. W. (1983). *American minority relations,* New York: Alfred A. Knopf.

Wadman, R.C., & Allison, W.T. (2004). *To protect and to serve a history of police in America.* Upper Saddle River, N.J.: Prentice Hall.

Walker, S. (1983). *The police in America.* New York: McGraw-Hill.

Walker, S. (1997). "Complaints against the police: A focus group study of citizen perceptions, goals, and expectations," *Criminal Justice Review* 22 (2), 207–225.

Walker, S., Spohn, C., & Delone, M. (2000). *The color of justice.* Wadsworth: Belmont, C.A.

Wallace, H., Robertson C., & Steckler, C. (2001)). *Written & interpersonal communication methods for law enforcement* (2nd ed). Upper Saddle River, NJ: Prentice Hall.

Weisburg, D., & Greenspan, R. (2002). *Police attitudes toward abuse of authority: Findings from a national study.* National Institute of Justice Research in Brief.

Westley, W. (1970). *Violence and the Police.* Cambridge: Massachusetts Institute of Technology.

Whisenand, P.M., & Ferguson, R.F. (2002). *The managing of police organizations* (5th ed.). Upper Saddle River, NJ: Prentice Hall.

Wilson, J. Q. (1968). *Varieties of police behavior: The management of law and order in eight communities.* Cambridge, MA: Harvard University Press.

CHAPTER 7

Navigating Historical Cross-Cultural Antecedents of Crime Theory and Control

Concetta C. Culliver and Francisca O. Norales

A CHANGING SOCIETY

Importantly, almost everywhere today, nations continue to be concerned about crime reduction tactics: their quest is to know what works and what doesn't and what is working for other nations. Schmalleger (2006) commenting on "globalization" and "comparative criminology" believes that there is a consensus that society is experiencing considerable change that appears fundamentally different from what has occurred in past decades. Crime, including cross-national criminality, is no exception to this focus. In fact, in his views on comparative criminology, Schmalleger (2006) strongly concedes that the crime globalization problem has definitely rekindled high interest in comparative criminology, or what he sees as a cross-national perspective about the study of crime. Also, when analyzing and comparing crime patterns of one country to those of another, the crime causation theories and policies that have been highly acknowledged in one jurisdiction can be re-evaluated in the light of world experience. Interestingly, some renowned criminologists have observed that the challenge for comparative criminologists is to develop theories with increased specificity while managing to construct them so that they can be applied across more than one culture or nation-state. (Howard, Newman, & Pridemore cited in Schmalleger, 2006).

HISTORICAL ASPECTS OF COMPARATIVE CRIMINOLOGY

Schmalleger (2006) remarked that "globalization of knowledge" has been widely used to illustrate one's increased understanding that results from information sharing across cultures, and that cross-cultural knowledge is beginning to play a significant role in the criminological theory process and the development of American crime control policies. Howard, et al. (2004) suggested the following: "Globalization will make it increasingly difficult for nation states to ignore the criminal justice information of other countries. Politicians and influential bureaucrats increasingly will be forced to explain why their country displays crime rates, prosecution rates, incarceration rates, or rates of violence or gun ownership that are strikingly different from those of similar countries" (Schmalleger, 2006, p. 540). Also, with a comparative criminological approach to the study of cross-cultural and cross-national crime and crime prevention and control, the American system of criminal justice has made and continues to make tremendous advancements. Though not a new phenomenon, its rudiments were noticed when, in the fifth century B.C., the Romans experienced a serious crime wave and found it necessary to send a team of delegates to the more advanced nation of Greece for training in crime control.

Reflections on many cross-cultural and cross-national perspectives of crime and punishment have permeated both the American and European systems of criminal justice and criminology down through the years, especially as related to the Age of Reason, or the Enlightenment, when medieval beliefs that God directly was in control of all human behavior and that the church's authority was never to be questioned, were challenged (Barkan, 2006; Schmalleger, 2006). René Descartes, John Locke, and Jean Jacques Rousseau were all Enlightenment philosophers who strongly believed that God had endowed individuals with the means to govern their own affairs through the service of free will and reason.

A BRIEF HISTORY OF THE CLASSICAL SCHOOL OF CRIMINOLOGY

Within criminology, this enlightenment led to the advent of the Classical School of Criminological Thought, where individuals were seen as having control over their behavior, such that any criminality engaged in could be explained as a particularly individualized form of evil or more specifically, as immoral behavior fueled by one's own personal choice. Two renowned philosophers emerged as classical school criminologists: Cesar Beccaria, an Italian economist, and an English philosopher, Jeremy Bentham. Both made meaningful contributions that had and continue to have a profound impact on American and many European criminal justice systems.

Widely regarded as the father of modern criminology who published a path-breaking book on crime and punishment, Beccaria empowered himself to effectuate many changes within the reigns of the classical school, changes engendered by his treatise that led to numerous reforms in the criminal courts and prisons. Interestingly, one admirer referred to him as "prophet" of an enlightened approach involving crime prevention and crime control (Mueller, 1990). Even critics of Beccaria's ideas and reforms marveled at the tremendous degree of influence that his views had across Europe. Beccaria's ideas also impacted the thinking of John Adams, Benjamin Franklin, and Thomas Jefferson as well.

Jeremy Bentham, the other renowned figure of the classical school, like Beccaria, believed that individuals weigh the facts about intended criminality in terms of pleasure or pain and that the law itself was far more severe than it needed to be for rational individuals to be deterred from behaving criminally. Barkan (2006) noted how Bentham's writings produced changes in the English criminal law in the early 1800's and assisted in the development of the first modern police force in 1829, the London Metropolitan Police Department. In addition, his writings led to the creation of a modern prison. However, prior to the time of Bentham, Beccaria, and other legal reformers, long-term imprisonment was non-existent. Jails did exist but were intended only for suspects awaiting trial, torture, or execution, and such stays were of short duration (Barkan, 2006; Hunter & Dantzker, 2002; Reid, 2000; Schmalleger,

2006). According to Hunter and Dantzker (2002), the main premises of
the classical school of criminology are as follows:

1. The social contract, whereby an individual is obligated to
   society only by his or her own consent and, likewise, society
   is responsible to the citizen.
2. Free will — individuals have the freedom to make their
   own choices to act.
3. Individuals will seek pleasure and avoid pain.
4. Punishment should be used only as a deterrent to criminal
   behavior.
5. The seriousness of the crime should be the basis for
   punishment.
6. Punishment for identical crimes should not be different,
   but identical.

The "social contract" concept attributed to the work of Beccaria,
implying a two-way commitment between the individual and society,
means that strong adherence to laws enacted by societal legislative bodies
is expected. In turn, agents of social control (police, court, corrections)
have the responsibility to provide fair and equitable treatment in exchange
for citizen compliance. Further, failure on the part of state government
officials to treat its citizens properly, negates the social contract.

Of great importance are two additional concepts of the classical school
of thought surrounding crime and punishment: equity and due process.
By equity, classical philosophers and criminologists, including Beccaria
and Bentham, purported to mean that laws should be applied equally to
all citizens regardless of social status. Moreover, matters such as race,
class, religion, gender, or ideology including political, are not to influence
the administration of justice. Therefore, when the state breeches its contract
to provide fair and equitable treatment, then this could result in dismissal
of charges against the accused. Also, when chronic failure is noted on
the part of the state to provide fair and equitable treatment to its citizens,
this too, could result in total distrust of the system and social contract
nullification (Beccaria, 1963; Bentham, 1948; Dantzker & Hunter, 2002).

With the concept "due process," every citizen charged with violation of the criminal law is to be accorded the full protection of the law during investigation, including interrogation, prosecution, and adjudication. With due process the accused is to be presumed innocent until proved otherwise, and the accused should not be subjected to punishment prior to guilt having been legally established (Schmalleger, 2006). Equally important is that sanctions imposed on the accused must be mandated through the principles of both Beccaria and Bentham, and in accordance with legal proscriptions (Beccaria, 1963; Bentham, 1789; Schmalleger, 2006). As with breeches involving equity, failure to adhere to one's due process rights could lead to "acquittal" for the defendant. At the same time, chronic failures could seriously impair the state's ability to govern (Hunter and Dantzker, 2002).

THE NEOCLASSICAL SCHOOL

Flourishing during the 19th Century, the neoclassical school maintained the same basis as did the classical school of criminology in the belief of "free will," meaning that one's behavior is governed by "choice" and "rational thinking." Any rationality beyond choice or free will to explain one's criminality was totally disregarded. However, after closer analysis concerning application of classical criminology during the eighteenth century, flaws were observed with regard to ideas and rationales about "identical punishment" for "identical crimes," as well as with the concepts of both "free will" and "rationality." With the focus shifted from the "criminal act" to the "criminal man," it was noted that aggravating or mitigating circumstances sometimes caused similar crimes to differ in various and significant ways. Additionally, though the concept of free will was not abandoned, criminologists and philosophers acknowledged and realized that there were moments and circumstances whereby "limited freedom of choice" would exist. This, consequently, led many nations, including the United States that had been implementing classical criminology, to amend their ideas (Vold et al. 1998). Such changes in classical criminology developed into "Neo-Classical Criminology." Criminology systems based on neoclassical school tenets and integrating neoclassical revision had to consider the following: mitigating and aggravating circumstances; youth; insanity; necessity; duress; self-defense; and to lesser degrees, ignorance of the law and intoxication (Lilly et al.1995; Liska & Messner, 1999; Reid, 2000; Roberson & Wallace, 1998).

"JUST DESERTS" AND NEOCLASSICAL CRIMINOLOGY: RECEIVING DESERVED PUNISHMENT

In recent years neoclassical school advocates have deemed it necessary to revisit the importance of the "social contract" when administering punishment (Hunter & Dantzker, 2002). With the perception of a failed rehabilitation system, scholars have argued that punishment is essential for criminals and that their own actions demand that criminal sanctions be applied. Both the offenders' culpability and the seriousness of crimes strongly mandate the need for and application of punishment (Adler, Mueller, & Laufer, 1998).

The basic idea of the "just deserts" argument is that even if specific deterrence — preventing particular offenders from engaging in repeated criminality — is not achieved, society still needs assurance that criminals receive deserved punishment; failure to apply deserved punishment would be a violation of the social contract and would also erode respect for law and authority (Schmalleger, 2006).

THE CURRENT STATUS OF THE CLASSICAL SCHOOL

Overall, the classical or neoclassical thought is more representative of a philosophy of justice than of a crime causation theory according to Martin et al. (1990). Moreover, the influences of Beccaria and the Enlightenment, as well as views of other classical thinkers, continue to have tremendous influence on the American system of justice. For example, the U.S. Constitution with the existing "get-tough" approaches to crime and punishment and the continuing emphasis on individual rights, are legacies of the Classical School in which the nation can be reminded in almost all dimensions of the present-day criminal justice system (Ibid.). Also, advocates of contemporary neoclassical approaches to crime control and prevention, without hesitation, credit themselves for the recent decline in crime rates, especially with the enactment of determinate sentencing. Determinate sentencing mandated by state legislative bodies requires certain types of offenders who commit certain types of crimes to be given a prison sentence with a minimum amount of time designated. The laws governing determinate sentencing give neither Judges nor prosecutors any discretionary power to alter this mandated sentencing strategy. Habitual offender laws stipulate that after an offender accrues a certain number of convictions, usually two or three major felony convictions, the offender is to receive a lengthy prison term, usually for life, and sometimes without the possibility of parole. The "Three Strikes and You're Out" law is an example germane to mandatory sentencing. (Shelden and Brown, 2003; Sigler and Culliver, 1988).

THE POSITIVE SCHOOL OF CRIMINOLOGY: A CROSS-CULTURAL PERSPECTIVE

Reid (2000) lamented that fashions and fads of human thought impact many fields and that criminology is no exception. With this analogy, Reid's implications are suggestive of philosophical shifts that occur with crime and punishment from time to time, some of which are politically fueled. For example, during the 18th century the major emphasis was on a punishment philosophy which lost strength in the following century. Until the slight shift from the classical to the neoclassical school of criminological thought, no emphasis was on crime-causation theory, as the main focus was only on the "criminal act".

As for positivist criminology, the late 18th century made significant advances in understanding both the physical and social causes of crime. The French Sociologist, Auguste Comte (1798–1857), upon application of modernized methods of the physical sciences to social sciences, argued that for real knowledge of social phenomena to be accepted and recognized, a positive, scientific approach was a must. Then came the advancements of others such as Darwin's theory of evolution whereby old and obsolete ideas that demons and animal spirits could explain human behavior were replaced with knowledge based on sound new scientific principles, thus moving the field of criminology from a philosophical to a scientific perspective.

Although it was during the 19th century that major biological theories to explain criminal behavior came into being, still their origins were noted much earlier. For instance, one Greek scientist in pursuit of the relationship between biological traits and behavior, upon examination of Socrates' skull and facial features, found them to resemble those of a person with an inclination toward alcoholism and brutality (Ellis, 1900).

THE THEORY OF ATAVISM

Lombroso (1918), through his theory of atavism (born criminal concept), asserted that criminals are born, not made, and that their behavior results from primitive urges. Such criminals were believed to be evolutionary accidents or throwbacks to primitive society (Hunter & Dantzker, 2002). Yet, the born criminal philosophy, according to Adler, et al. (2001), has an even earlier historical dimension suggesting that criminals are born, and that identification is possible by various physical irregularities. Shakespeare in Julius Caesar stated:

> Let me have men about me that are fat; sleek-headed
> men, and such as sleep a nights. Yond Cassius has a
> lean and hungry look; he thinks too much; such men
> are dangerous. (cited in Adler et al. 2001, p. 67).

Although its roots date back to ancient times, it was during the sixteenth century that Italian physician Giambattista della Porta (1535–1615) founded the school of human physiognomy, the study of the relationship of facial features and human behavior. Several centuries later, Porta's efforts were rekindled by Swiss theologian Johann Kaspas Lavater (1741–1801). This was elaborated on through the efforts of the German physicians Frank Joseph Gall (1758–1828) and Johann Kaspar Spurzheir (1776–1832), whose science of phrenology confirmed that bumps on the head were indicative of psychological propensities, including a proneness to criminality (Mannheim, 1965). Lombroso (1918), after studying Italian criminals (post mortem studies of bodies of executed and deceased offenders), was able to reinforce the belief that most criminals are predisposed to criminality (Schmalleger, 2006). Meanwhile, so popularly recognized as the positive school of criminology, much credit is attributed to Italian physician, Cesare Lombroso, who is highly recognized as the "Father of Scientific Criminology." Strong supporters of the positive school of thought firmly believed that external forces such as biological, psychological, and sociological ones generated criminal behavior. This rejects the legal concept of crime as recognized by the classical school with its focus on the criminal act. Positive criminologists focused on the individual and sought scientific support for this criminological approach to ascertain crime causation. Accommodating this major shift was an emphasis on treatment rather than punishment.

DETERMINISM: POSITIVE CRIMINOLOGY

Determinism, one of the basic underpinnings of positive criminology, asserts that forces exist beyond one's control (including biological and cultural ones) that determine, govern, and define human behavior. According to Gaines, Kaune, & Miller, (2000), the three types of determinism include: 1) grim determinism, the belief that God has ordained certain behaviors and nothing can stifle or prevent them from occurring. This perspective maintained prevalence during ancient and medieval times; 2) hard determinism, the view that behavior has a birth-programmatic linkage. It is primarily natural (e.g., biological) and allows for no or only limited free will; and 3) soft determinism, which sees behavior as having biological (nature) or sociological (nurture) characteristics. In this instance, one's freedom of choice is limited by nature and / or nurture.

Aside from Lombroso's (1918) ideas about atavism that assert the born-criminal concept, other criminal offender types as indicated by Schmalleger (2006), are as follows:

1. The insane criminal: those considered to be mental and moral degenerates, alcoholics, drug addicts, and so on.

2. The criminaloid type criminal: also known as the occasional criminal, whose criminality was said to have been fueled by environmental factors; some exhibited behavior elements associated with atavism (to some degree) even though they are said to differ from the born criminal type.

3. The passion criminal type: those who engage in criminal behavior by virtue of passion and have surrendered to intense emotions including love, jealousy, hatred, or a shattered or injured sense of honor.

4. As for the "criminal woman" type, Lombroso (1918) believed that criminal behavior among women, as found with men, was derived from an atavistic foundation. In addition, violence among women was interpreted and explained within the framework of the "Masculinity Hypothesis" theory, or the belief that masculine features and mannerisms were associated with criminal women (Culliver, 1993; Schmalleger, 2006).

COMMUNICATING THROUGH THE AMERICAN AND EUROPEAN JUSTICE SYSTEMS

Lombroso (1918) exposed and supported additional ideas which are in full force today with the American system of criminal justice as well as with the European criminal justice systems. The idea of shorter prison sentences was rejected, because it was believed that shorter-term periods of incarceration only served to expose inmates to other offenders and, therefore, left little or no time for rehabilitation. Alternatives to incarceration such as home confinement, judicial reprove, fines, forced labor, local exiles, corporal punishment, and the conditional sentence were strongly advocated. Use of probation, which was noted as being effective in the United States, was advocated. Only as a last resort was the death penalty supported. Furthermore, use of restitution for crime victims, widely used today as an expression of high regard for "restorative justice" or "reparative justice" was highly regarded. Moreover, Lombroso was a champion of crime prevention (Reid, 2000).

INTERCULTURAL KNOWLEDGE ACQUISITION

Laying the foundation for knowledge acquisition of crime causation through scientific discovery, other criminologists, sociologists, and psychologists representing Europe and the United States commenced their quest to support or refute already created theories such as the following: The English medical officer, Charles Buckman Goring (1870–1919), for example, challenged Lombroso's (1918) "born criminal" hypothesis using prisoners in England. German psychiatrist, Ernst Kretschmer (1888–1964), investigated the link between physical characteristics and crime while Richard Dugdale (1841–1883) studied descendants of Ada Jukes known as the mother of criminals in search of "inherited criminality linkage."

In a similar vein, Henry Goddard (1866–1957) studied descendants of the Kallikak family to substantiate the inherited criminality connection. He found a link to feeblemindedness, but not to criminality (Schmalleger, 2006). Isaac Ray (1807–1881), for example, is acknowledged as America's first forensic psychiatrist and maintained throughout his lifetime a sincere interest in the application of psychiatric principles involving the law. Authoring the "Medical Jurisprudence of Insanity" (his treatise on criminal responsibility), Ray (1838) defended the concept of moral insanity, which was initially described in 1806 by French psychiatrist and humanitarian Philippe Pinel (1745–1826) to characterize individuals who behaved normally, with the exception of the areas of the brain that regulates affective responses. Ray's concern was with the legality of holding one responsible for his or her acts, including criminality, when one should have such impairment and be engaged in criminal behavior without "actus reus"or the criminal intent to do so. Interestingly, the English medical professor Henry Maudsley (1835–1918) shared Ray's (1938) concerns about criminal responsibility. He suggested that for many individuals, crime is an outlet in which their illogical tendencies are released and that if they were not criminals they would go mad. Most of Maudley's attention concerned the borderline between insanity and criminal behavior.

Sigmund Freud (1856–1938), a Viennese physician, is credited with having made the greatest contribution to the development of psychoanalytic theory. Adopting the idea of the unconscious, he argued that some behavior could be explained with reference to early childhood traumatic experiences, and that such experiences leave a mark on the individual that is buried in the unconscious. Freud further contended that the mind is comprised of three levels: conscious, preconscious, and unconscious. The conscious mind is that aspect of the mind that involves "awareness," such as one's daily thoughts. The preconscious mind contains elements of experiences that are outside of one's awareness but can be brought back to consciousness at any time, through memories and experiences. The unconscious part of the mind is where biological desires and urges that cannot readily be experienced as thoughts are stored. Freud alluded to "repression" and explained that part of the unconscious contains feelings about sex and hostility, which through the process of "repression," one could keep below the surface of consciousness (Martin et al., 1990). Freud later categorized his ideas of the conscious and unconscious into three categories: the id, which consists of those powerful urges and drives for instant gratification and satisfaction; the ego that acts as moderator between the superego and id; and the superego, which serves as a moral guide to right and wrong and acts as a moral code or conscience.

The social determinant factors of criminal behavior are what scholars during the 19th and early 20th centuries directed their attention to. The Belgian Mathematician Adolphe Quetelet (1796–1874) and French lawyer André Michel Guerry (1802–1866) were among the first scholars to repudiate the classical school "free will doctrine." Analyzing crime statistics in relationship to such factors as poverty, age, sex, race, and climate, these researchers concluded that societal factors rather than decisions of individual offenders proved responsible for criminality. Moreover, publishing the first modern criminal statistics in France in 1827, Guerry (2001) used those published statistics to illustrate that crime rates are influenced and fueled by social factors. He discovered that the wealthiest region of France contained the highest rate of property crime, but a decreased national rate of violent crime, concluding that property crime was heavily associated with "opportunity"; in the more affluent areas, there was much more to steal.

Using the countries of France, Belgium, and Holland, Quetelet (1842) engaged in a more detailed analysis of crime, which he termed "moral statistics," and concluded that by observing the overall behavior patterns of groups within society as a whole, consistency would be noted with regard to crime statistics of various crime typologies. In the publication, "A Treatise of Man," Quetelet (1842) further remarked:

> We can enumerate in advance how many individuals will soil their hands in the blood of their fellows, how many will be frauds, how many prisoners; almost as one can enumerate in advance the births and deaths that will take place (cited in Adler et al., 2001 p. 75).

With a focus on groups rather than individuals, Quetelet (1842) discovered that behavior is undeniably predictable, regular, and comprehensible, and concluded that human behavior is governed by external forces. Therefore, the more criminologists learn about such forces, the easier it would be to predict one's criminality. Thus, Quetelet proposed that criminologists first identify factors related to crime and then associate such factors based on the extent by which one's criminal behavior is influenced by the identified factors. Though neither Quetelet nor Guerry provided a theory of criminality, they both introduced the idea of studying social factors that influence crime scientifically.

Gabriel Tarde (1843–1904), who had served as a French provincial judge and then later as head of France's national statistics, formulated one of the earliest sociological theories of criminal behavior, using France's national statistical system. His extensive investigation concluded the following:

> The majority of murderers and notorious thieves began as children who had been abandoned, and the true seminary of crime must be sought for upon each public square or each crossword of our towns, whether they be small or large, in those flocks of pillaging street urchins who, like bands of sparrows, associate together,

at first for marauding, and then for theft, because of a lack of education and food in their homes. (cited in Adler et al., 2001, p. 76).

In essence, Tarde (1907) rejected Lombroso's (1918) theory of biological abnormalities of crime causation and argued that criminal offenders were normal individuals who had only learned criminality, similar to other learned legitimate trade tactics, (Adler et al., 2001). From this stance, Tarde framed the theory of crime according to "laws of imitation," principles governing the process by which individuals become criminals, believing that individuals emulate behavior in much the manner that they mimic styles of dress (Adler et al., 2001). Tarde (1907) expounded on the three-fold theory as follows: (1) behavior imitation is done in proportion to intensity and contact frequency; (2) behavior imitation is about inferior imitating superiors, or that trends flow from town to country and from upper classes to lower classes; and (3) when a clash occurs between two behavior patterns, one may occupy the place of the other, as for example, when knives were replaced to a great extent by guns as murder weapons. Of great importance is that Tarde's work proved foundational for Edwin Sutherland's renowned theory of differential association relevant to learned (imitational) behavior (Adler et al., 2001).

Of all the nineteenth-century scholars who had researched the relationship between crime and social factors, none has more powerfully impacted contemporary criminology as than Emile Durkheim. In fact, Durkheim is recognized as one of the founders of sociology. He directly experienced major societal ills and chaos, when at the age of 12, he witnessed his hometown, Epinal, in Eastern France invaded and occupied by the German Army. The effects and societal changes resulting from this invasion preoccupied him throughout his lifetime. Interestingly, at the age of 29, Durkheim became a professor at the University of Bordeaux, where he taught his first course in sociology and later relocated to the University of Paris where he completed his doctorial studies. His "Division of Social Labor" became a milestone in that it centered on societal organization (Adler et al., 2001).

According to Durkheim (1938), crime is a normality of society. He further noted that theoretically, crime could cease altogether only if societal members had the same values. However, he rationalized this type of standardization to be neither possible nor desirable. In fact, the following is proposed:

> The opportunity for the genius to carry out his work affords the criminal his originality at a lower level... According to Athenian laws, Socrates was a criminal, and his condemnation was no more than just. However, his crime, namely, the independence of his thought, rendered a service not only to humanity but to his country (as cited in Adler et al., 2001, p. 77).

Durkheim (1938) further remarked that societies have not only crime but sanctions accompanying criminal behavior, and that such sanctions varied according to societal structure. In a society where there is strong cohesiveness, members who become law violators would be punished. Durkheim went further to extol the idea of punishment since it is the mechanism to buttress societal values — to remind individuals of the rights and wrongs necessary for societal preservation and solidarity. Punishment, Durkheim lamented, must be harsh; must take into consideration the wrong done to crime victims; and must adhere to use of restitution along with immediate restoration of order. One of the most praiseworthy efforts of Durkheim's many contributions to contemporary sociology and criminology is the concept of "anomie," the breakdown of social order or feelings of formlessness and apathy resulting from a collapse of social cohesion when individuals are unable to cope with societal changes that result from a loss of standards and values. Stated more simply, when a society is plagued by anomie, then societal cohesion will be replaced by disintegration, turmoil, confusion, and chaos.

THE JUVENILE JUSTICE SYSTEM
AND THE DOCTRINE OF PARENS PATRIAE

When discussing or examining the juvenile justice, it is vital to consider its origins and the evolution of the *parens patriae* doctrine, meaning that the state would stand in place of the parent (*en loco parentis*) to govern the behavior of delinquent children. Classified as status offenders are those whose delinquent behaviors include juvenile curfew violation, running away from home, school truancy, and others; and those whose behavior is in violation of the state's penal code including larceny-theft, burglary, aggravated assault, and others.

According to Jackson and Knepper (2003), *parens patriae* involves intervention by authority imposed on those who are unable or unwilling to make acceptable decisions or whose decisions are in direct violation of the penal code. Also, the major premise of *parens patriae* is its political linkage to society, along with child rearing practices. Consequently, the *parens patriae* doctrine has historically mandated and promoted a specific perception of parenthood that provides acceptable or unacceptable standards for childrearing.

While the *parens patriae* philosophy was the main thrust and foundation of the American System of Juvenile Justice established in Cook Co. Illinois in 1899, its origin has been traced back to Ancient Babylonia. For example, during the eighteenth century B.C., King Hammurabe of Babylonia established a set slate of laws for citizens in order to bring about social order. Criminologists consider The Hammurabic code to be the first written laws (Allen & Simonsen, 1992). *Parens Patriae* emanated from these established social control laws, of which at the time the political environment centered on conservative ideology with a prevailing tone of societal protection. Today, this would equate with America's "get tough" approach to crime and delinquency or what can be referred to as "just deserts" (Schmalleger, 2006).

More specifically, children received harsh punishment, and the laws did not separate the delinquent's acts of children from the criminal acts of adults (Jackson & Knepper, 2003). Children whose delinquent acts were even minor in nature were treated as adults; they were not separated from adults in prisons, nor were they rendered any preferential treatment. If the act was punishable by sanction (specifically stated law), then punitive measures, hanging included, were based solely on the act itself, with no consideration of the offender's age. No clear distinctions under King Hammurabi of Babylonia's code of law distinguished the most serious (felony offenses) from the less serious crimes (misdemeanors). Additional specifications of the *parens patriae* doctrine of the Hammurabic code included children being severely punished for disobedience to parents and for failure to attend school. Status offenses, as indicated by Jackson and Knepper (2003), were dealt with immediately. In other words, the punishment was "swift and certain," ranging from whippings to mutilations. Because children were expected to be very obedient to parents, the father in the Babylonia era played a key role in the family. The father was not only viewed and regarded as head of the household, but also as the prime punisher when the child behaved improperly. Of great interest is the notion of granting fathers unlimited and unquestionable control over their children. Indeed, the child-rearing practice that evolved into a central notion of *parens patriae*, evolved from an early Roman principle called *patria potestas*.

Patria Potestas
Both the Greek and Roman empires contributed considerably to the concept of *parens patriae*. The Greeks as a democratic civilized society promoted individualism, freedom, protection of rights and due process. Much of the political ideology, the framework as well as philosophies relevant to government and family, continue to be borrowed from ancient Greek culture (Jackson & Knepper, 2003). Further, Draconian laws concerning issues of crime and punishment about juvenile justice and delinquency continue to be of major concern to criminologists. While the fifth and sixth centuries B.C. in ancient Greek history reflected a culturally intellectual and just society, matters changed during the seventh century with the Athenian statesmen and lawmaker, Draco. Draco instituted and imposed legal codes, using sanctions and punishments that were severe, harsh, and consisted of beatings, public mutilations, and even death (Jackson & Knepper, 2003).

The Roman Law and Juveniles

Under the Roman law, individual rights and due process prevailed. Roman law itself descends from a written code known as the Twelve Tables (Abadinski, 1991). With this code of law, fathers had absolute power and control over their families. They could sell family members, children included, into slavery and could beat and mutilate their children. With *patria potestas*, the father's absolute power over his family to the Romans was indicative of the power of life and death. The concept *patria potestas* was somewhat modified upon its adoption by English kings and translated into the English common law system. However, with England's lack of a constitution, it is still bound by the English common law system (Jackson & Knepper, 2003).

The Impact of the English Common Law System in America

America's System of Juvenile Justice has been tremendously impacted by both ancient Roman law and English common law. While the tradition of fathers having authority over families followed the English common law, this tradition in England was not absolute due to factors associated with English culture such as the king, the Church of England, and matters pertaining to punishing children. In England it was the king, not fathers, who was noted as divine authority not only over children, but over the entire country. Simply stated, the king assumed royal power and authority over every citizen (Jackson & Knepper, 2003) thus engendering the need for England to rewrite the Roman laws to reflect and depict justice in the name of His Majesty. The monarch's authority kindled great concern in the Church of England when royal sovereigns attempted to claim dominance over the church. Nonetheless, the king's law reigned universal or common throughout England and tapped every aspect of life. English common law includes all customs and traditions used for decision-making by the English courts.

More specifically, the king seized ultimate power as guardian over the lives of children who were considered his wards. It was during this period that the idea of *parens patriae* was clarified and interpreted by the king to permit intervention into the lives of children whenever necessary, legitimate, and just. Under English common law, though families were responsible for their children, the king maintained responsibility for subjects through *parens patriae*. As father of the country, he assumed responsibility for the protection and behavior of children and to oversee their needs particularly when family conflict and disintegration occurred. Monarchs assumed this responsibility with zealousness, especially when wealthy families were affected, because the kingdom could inherit the wealth when children become wards of the sovereign.

Use of *parens patriae* was challenged in England through the 1927 Wellesley vs. Wellesley case (Jackson & Knepper, (2003). This case involved the court of Chancery making the decision to allow the Duke of Beaufort's children to be placed with their aunt upon the death of their mother (Duke's wife). It had been the mother's final request that their father, the Duke of Beaufort, not be granted custody of the children due to history of an adulterous affair and his relocation to Paris with her, thereby creating separation between the Duke, his wife and children. The court ruled in favor of the children's maternal aunt receiving custody of the children instead of their father, who would have been granted custody under Roman *patria potestas*. The court's decision used as its basis: "best interest of the children," reflecting *parens patriae* that had been passed from the Roman *patria potestas* and interpreted legally by the English Chancery court as follows:

> The Court of Chancery has jurisdiction to appoint a guardian for infants, being Wards of the Court, excluding the father; and upon evidence that the father was living in a state of adultery, and had encouraged his children in swearing, keeping low company, etc. {sic}, it was held a fit case to exercise the power to exclude him from the guardianship (cited in Jackson & Knepper, 2003, p. 6).

Unquestionably, traces of Roman law prevailed throughout colonial America as well as today in contemporary American society reflecting, for example, one of the basic tenets of the crime control model — "guilty until proven innocent" with its basis in Roman law. However, according to English common law where due process prevails, one is presumed innocent until proven guilty. Consequently, current examples of the *parens patriae* depict integration of both Roman and English law into the contemporary U.S. legal structure (Jackson & Knepper, 2003 p. 6).

Contemporary Interpretations of Parens Patriae

Although some erosion of the *parens patriae* doctrine has occurred over the past three or four decades, Johnston and Secret (1995) reported it to have been very lively and active during the 1990's. This doctrine's persistence is evidenced by the various dispositional options available to juvenile court judges and others involved in the earlier stages of processing juveniles through the juvenile justice system. Most dispositional options are either nominal or conditional, and confinement is sanctioned only as a last resort. With nominal or conditional options, the sanctions are relatively mild: for example, verbal warning or strong reprimand, diversion, probation, financial restitution to victim, community service, individual or group therapy, or even education programming. These sanctions, according to Mershon (1991), reflect the rehabilitation or medical model ideology that has been a major underpinning of *parens patriae*.

However, strong adherence to the rehabilitative orientation which permeates the *parens patriae* concept is conflicting with contemporary juvenile justice ideals of accountability, justice, and due process. Contemporary juvenile court jurisprudence now mandates individual accountability for one's actions. Increasingly, the current trend leans more in the direction of "just deserts" and justice in the American Juvenile Justice System. In addition, the current mode reflects a "get tough" approach that is geared toward punishment that is swift, certain, and harsh. According to Gordon (1990), the previously adopted rehabilitative philosophy of juvenile justice promoted greater use of nonsecure, secure and incarcerative sanctions in state-operated group homes, industrial schools, or even reform schools. For juveniles charged and adjudicated for serious violent offenses, current laws mandate transfer to adult criminal court jurisdiction.

Additional factors that currently impact the *parens patriae* doctrine include the constitutional rights of juveniles as well as the changing role of juvenile court prosecutors. Since the mid-1960's, juveniles have acquired greater constitutional rights that are more commensurate with those afforded to adults in criminal courts: for example, right to counsel and right to face one's accuser. As juveniles are vested with increased numbers of constitutional rights, the likelihood of a juvenile court depicting greater criminalization will emanate (Johnston & Secret, 1995).

With regard to the role of juvenile court prosecutors, greater transformation will continue to occur as prosecutors become involved in pursuing cases against juvenile defendants, causing criminologists to perceive a weakened and strained delinquency prevention focus, necessary to deter youths from further criminality, including adult criminal behavior. Although prosecutors, more often than not, operate with the intention to ensure due process entitlements to juvenile offenders, there are social costs attached in that the youths are labeled in such ways that they become more propelled toward criminality than away from it (Ellsworth, Kinsella, & Massin, 1992).

CONCLUSIONS

The development of the theory on crime, punishment, and crime control in the United States and in Europe has as its foundation a rich, historical, cross-national and a cross-cultural legacy. This development does not only encompass Greek, Roman, and English common law criminology, but is reflected in contemporary American criminological systems.

Clearly, nations have been and continue to be interdependent. No one nation can exist or survive on its own. So is it imperative that nations continue to seek understanding of other cultures in interacting and communicating globally.

REFERENCES

Abadinski, A. (1991). *Law and justice.* Chicago: Nelson-Hall.

Adler, F., Mueller, G.O.W., & Laufer, W.S. (2001). *Criminology.* Boston: McGraw-Hill.

Adler, F., Mueller, G.O.W. & Laufer, W.S. (1998). *Criminology,* 3rd ed. Boston: McGraw-Hill.

Allen, H., & Simonsen, C. (1992). *Corrections in America* (6th ed.). New York: Macmillan.

Barkan, S. (2006). *Criminology a sociological understanding.* Upper Saddle River, New Jersey: Prentice-Hall.

Barlow, H.D. (2000). *Criminal justice in America.* Upper Saddle River, NJ: Prentice-Hall.

Beccaria, C. (1963). Essay on crimes and punishments. Translated with an introduction by H. Paolucci. New York: Macmillan. In F. Schmalleger, (Ed.), *Criminology today an integrated approach.* Upper Saddle River, New Jersey: Prentice-Hall.

Bentham, J. (1948). An introduction to the principles of morals and legislation: In R.D. Hunter and M.L. Dantzker (Eds.). *Crime and criminality.* Upper Saddle River, New Jersey: Prentice-Hall.

Bentham, J. (1789). An introduction to the principles of morals and legislation (London: T. Payne, 1789). In F. Schmalleger, (Ed.), *Criminology today an integrative approach.* Upper Saddle River, New Jersey: Prentice-Hall.

Blustein, J. (1983). On the doctrine of parens patriae. *Criminal Justice Ethics*, 2 (2), 39–47.

Champion, D. (2001). *The juvenile justice system delinquency, processing, and the law.* Upper Saddle River, New Jersey: Prentice-Hall.

Comte, A. (1830–1842). Cours de philosophie posetive (Course in positive philosophy). In F. Adler, G. Mueller, & W. Laufer (Eds.), *Criminology* (p.66). Boston: McGraw-Hill.

Culliver, C.C. (1993). *Female criminality. The state of the art.* New York: Garland Publishing, Inc.

Dugdale, R.L. (1895). The jukes: A study in crime pauperism, disease, and heredity. In F. Adler, G.Mueller, & W. Laufer (Eds.), *Criminology* (pp. 73–74). Boston: McGraw-Hill.

Durkheim, E. (1938). The rules of sociological method. In F. Adler, G. Mueller, & W. Laufer (Eds.), *Criminology* (pp. 76–77). Boston: McGraw-Hill.

Ellis, H. (1900). *The criminal*, 2nd ed. New York: Scribner.

Ellsworth, T., Kinsella, M., & Massin, K. (1992). "Prosecuting juveniles: Parens patriae and due process in the 1990's." *Justice Professional* 7: 53–67.

Fink, A. (1938). *The causes of crime: Biological theories in the United States, 1800–1915.* Philadelphia: University of Pennsylvania Press, p. 1.

Freud, S. (1920). A general introduction to psychoanalyses (New York: Liveright). In F. Adler., G. Mueller, etc. Laufer (Eds.), *Criminology* (pp. 87–88). Boston: McGraw-Hill.

Gaines, L.K., Kaune, M., & Miller, R.L. (2000). *Criminal justice in action.* Belmont, CA: Wadsworth.

Goddard, H., The Kallikak family: A study in the heredity of feeble-mindedness. In F. Adler, G. Mueller, & W. Laufer (Eds.), *Criminology* (p.74). Boston: McGraw-Hill.

Gordon, D.R. (1990). "The topography of criminal justice: A factor analysis of the get-tough policy trends. *Criminal Justice Policy Review:* 3: 184–207.

Goring, C. The English convict: A statistical study. In F. Adler, G. Mueller, & W. Laufer (Eds.), *Criminology* (p. 74). Boston: McGraw-Hill.

Guerry, A. (2001). In F. Adler, G. Mueller, & W. Laufer (Eds.), Criminology (p. 75). Boston: McGraw-Hill.

Howard, G., Newman, G., & Pridemore, W. "Theory, method and data in comparative criminology." In F. Schmalleger (Ed.), *Criminology today an integrative approach.* Upper Saddle River, New Jersey: Prentice-Hall.

Hunter, R. & Dantzker, M. (2002). *Crime & criminality.* Upper Saddle River, New Jersey: Prentice-Hall

Jackson, M.S., & Knepper, P. (2003). *Delinquency and justice a cultural perspective.* Boston: Pearson Education, Inc.

Johnson, J.B., & Secret, P.E. (1995). "The effects of court structure on juvenile court decision making: *Journal of Criminal Justice* 23: 63–82.

Kretschmer, E. (1926). *Physique and character.* New York: Harcourt Brace.

Lilly, J. R., Cullen, F.T., & Ball, R.A. (1995). *Criminological theory: Content and consequences,* 2nd ed. Thousand Oaks, CA: Sage.

Liska, A.E., & Messner, S.F. (1999). *Prospectives on crime and deviance*, 3rd ed. Upper Saddle River, NJ: Prentice-Hall.

Lombroso, C. (1918). Crime, its causes and remedies. Boston: Little Brown. In F. Adler, G.O.W. Mueller, W.S. Laufer (Eds.). *Criminology*. Boston: McGraw-Hill.

Mannheim, H. (1965). *Comparative criminology*. Boston: Houghton Mufflin.

Martin, R., Mutchnick, R.J., & Austin, W.T. (1990). *Criminological thought: Pioneers past and present*. New York: Macmillan.

Maudsley, H. In F. Adler, G. Mueller & W. Laufer (Eds.), *Criminology* (p. 74). Boston: McGraw-Hill.

Mershon, J.L. (1991). *Juvenile justice: The adjudicary and dispositional process*. Reno, NV: National Council of Juvenile and Family Court Judges.

Mueller, G.O.W. (1990). "Whose prophet is Cesare Becarria? An essay on the origins of criminological theory." In S. Barkan, (Ed.), *Criminology a sociological understanding*. Upper Saddle River, New Jersey: Prentice-Hall.

Pinel, P. (1806). A treatise on insanity. In F. Adler, G. Mueller, & W. Laufer (Eds.), *Criminology* (p. 74). Boston: McGraw-Hill.

Pisciotta, A.W. (1983a). Race, sex, and rehabilitation: A study in differential treatment in the juvenile reformatory. *Crime and Delinquency* 29 (2). 254–269.

Quetelet, A. (1842). A treatise on man in F.Adler G.Mueller, & W. Laufer (Eds.), *Criminology* (p. 75). Boston: McGraw-Hill.

Ray, I. (1838). The medical jurisprudence of insanity. In F. Adler, G. Mueller, & W. Laufer (Eds.), *Criminology* (p 74). Boston: McGraw-Hill.

Reid, S.T. (2000). *Crime and Criminology*, 9th ed. Boston: McGraw-Hill.

Roberson, C., & Wallace, H. (1998). *Introduction to criminology*. Incline Village, NV: Copperhouse.

Schmalleger, F. (2006). *Criminology today an integrative introduction*, 4th ed. Upper Saddle River NJ: Pearson Prentice-Hall.

Shelden, R.G., & Brown, W.B. (2003). *Criminal Justice in America*, Pearson Education, Inc.: Boston.

Sigler, R., & Culliver, C.C. (1988). Consequences of the habitual offender act on the costs of operating Alabama's Prisons, *Federal Probation.* Vol. LIT, no. 2.

Tarde, G. (1907). Social laws: An outline of sociology. In F. Adler, G. Mueller, & W. Laufer (Eds.), *Criminology* (p 76). Boston: McGraw-Hill.

Vold, G.B., Bernard, T. J., & Snipes, J.B. (1998). *Theoretical criminology,* 4th ed. New York: Oxford University Press.

CONTRIBUTORS

Francisca O. Norales, Ed.D., is Associate Professor of Business Information Systems at Tennessee State University in Nashville, TN. Among her many publications are *The Garífuna culture: A proclaimed masterpiece in Central America* (2003), *University students' learning efforts* (2003 and *Taking the right approach to diversity in the workplace* (1999). Dr. Norales is fluent in Garífuna.

Sister Marie Lorraine Bruno, M.A. Catholic University of America, and DLF, Institut Catholique de Paris, is an Associate Professor and former chairperson of Foreign Languages and Literatures at Immaculata University in Immaculata, PA. Sister Bruno is presently an emerita faculty and continues to teach a French language and a French literature course at Immaculata University.

A native of India, **Yash Garg** is the Director of Curriculum Materials Center at North Carolina Central University. She holds a Master's degree in English, Library Science, Educational Media, and Sanskrit. She has also taught Hindi and lectured on Indian culture at North Carolina State University.

Geraldine M. Norales is a Certified General Accountant in the province of Ontario, and has occupied managerial positions in the telecommunication industry in Ontario, Canada. Geraldine M. Norales, CGA is fluent in speaking Garífuna.

Concetta C. Culliver, Ed.D., Professor in CRJU at Coppin State University in Baltimore, MD. She has directed and administered several criminal justice programs including Murray State University, Murray, KY; Indiana University of Pennsylvania, Indiana, PA; Benedict College in Columbia, SC and Coppin State University in Baltimore, MD. Dr. Culliver has authored many articles and was the editor of the book, *Female criminality: The state of the art* (1993).

INDEX

A

A global company, 20
    visible minority, 63
American Civil Rights Movement, 31
Americans with Disabilities Act (ADA), 5
Arabian Sea, 27
automated teller machines (ATMs), 1

B

Beccaria, Cesar, 117
Bentham, Jeremy, 117
biculturalism, 59
bilingualism, 22, 59, 62
borderless world, 13, 14, 19, 26
Business Communication, v, 1, 6, 7, 12, 26

C

Cape of Good Hope, 29
Caribbean Sea, 46
Caribs, 47, 56
Challenge of Globalization, 13, 23
    see also globalization
    Awareness of the Need to Globalize, 20
    Changes in Organizations, 17
    cultural communication, x, xi, 14, 24
    Definition of Culture, 13, 31
    Emotional Challenges of Globalization, 18
    impact of globalization, the, 14
    Importance of Language, The, 14, 21
chipmaker, 2
chips, 2

see also Communicating within a multicultural workforce
in the banking sector, 65

E

Effective Business Communication, v
ethnocentric, xi

F

flexibility, 4, 11, 83, 84

G

Gandhi, Indira, 37
Gandhi, Mahatma, 30, 31, 33, 37
Garífuna Culture
    historical origin, x
    see also Proclamations by UNESCO
Garífuna-speaking People, 47, 48, 49, 54, 55
global community, 13, 18, 19
global marketplace, 11
globalization, ix, x, xi, 13, 14, 15, 16, 17, 18, 19, 20, 23, 115, 116
globalization of knowledge, xi, 116
globalize, 14
    the need, 20
guidelines
    when communicating, 8
Gupta dynasty, 29

H

Himalayan Mountains, 27
human rights considerations, ix, 56

I

improving intercultural and international relations, x
indigenous, 28
Intangible Heritage of Humanity, 45

P

Porter, John, 61, 66, 67

proclamations by UNESCO, ix, x, 45

Criteria used for selection: outstanding value, roots in cultural tradition, affirmation of cultural identity, source of inspiration and intercultural exchange, contemporary cultural and social role, excellence in the application of skills, unique testimo, ix

Masterpieces of the Oral and Intangible Heritage of Humanity, ix, 45

Purpose: outstanding cultural forms of expression to different countries of the world, ix

R

Relationship-Building Between the Police and Inner-City, African-American Minorities, 75

a relationship-building plan/suggestions, 98

citizen dissatisfaction, 84

Cyclical Poverty in Metropolitan Ghetto Regions, 76

improving relations with, 100

inner-city America, 75

juveniles' interaction with, 88

organizational change, 99

preservice/in-service training, 102

recruitment, screening, and selection, 101

strategies to achieve mutual respect, 105

the role, mission and duties, 79

training to improve relationship, 104

use of discretion, 83

Representing culture: Indian weddings, family, and festivals, 27

ancient history, 28

ceremonies, 35

culture defined, 31

family, 36

festivals, 38

www.ingramcontent.com/pod-product-compliance
Lightning Source LLC
Chambersburg PA
CBHW031600110426
42742CB00036B/567